An Introduction to Risk and Return from Common Stocks

An Introduction to Risk and Return from Common Stocks

Second Edition

R. A. Brealey

The MIT Press
Cambridge, Massachusetts

First MIT Press paperback edition, 1986

This book was set in Palatino by The MIT Press Computergraphics Department and printed and bound by The Murray Printing Co. in the United States of America.

Library of Congress Cataloging in Publication Data

Brealey, Richard A.
An introduction to risk and return from common stocks.

Bibliography: p.
1. Stocks. 2. Investment analysis. 3. Portfolio management. I. Title.
HG4661.B7 1983 332.63′223 82–23916
ISBN 0-262-02187-0 (hard)
0-262-52116-4 (paper)

To my wife

Contents

Preface

This book is intended for students and practicing investment managers. Its purpose is to describe briefly and simply the modern theory of investment management and some of the evidence underlying that theory.

It would be foolish to pretend that complex ideas can be fully explained in a short space, and often I have relied on intuitive arguments or dogmatic statements rather than proof. I hope nevertheless that the book manages to whet your appetite even if it does not fill your stomach.

When the first edition of *An Introduction to Risk and Return from Common Stocks* was published in 1969, systematic research into investment management was a recent innovation and had had little effect on the investment community. Since that time investment practice has been substantially influenced by these new ideas, and it is no longer possible for the manager of a large portfolio to ignore them.

This new edition reflects two other developments. First, there now exists a much more cohesive theoretical framework for thinking about investment problems. Second, there is now an abundance of new empirical studies of the behavior of stock prices, and this has compelled me to be much more selective in my choice of empirical evidence. I have for the most part described the classic studies rather than the most recent ones, but I have added a fairly extensive set of references for those readers who like to explore.

In summarizing the work of other financial economists I have incurred many debts. One of my greatest obligations is to the late Paul Cootner who encouraged me to write the original edition. I am also conscious of the pervasive influence that Jack Treynor has had on the ideas that are presented in this book, and to him I am especially grateful. Finally, I should like to thank Peter Bernstein, Elroy Dimson, Julian Franks, and William Sharpe for their many helpful comments on the manuscript.

I

The Reaction of Common Stock Prices to New Information

1 Technical Analysis and Random Walks

There are two kinds of security analysis. Fundamental analysis seeks to forecast each stock's return by studying the prospects for the company's business. Technical analysis attempts to forecast the return by searching for patterns in past stock prices.

Although a glance at any chart of past stock prices will often suggest such patterns, these could be no more than an optical illusion. Consider, for example, the following series of graphs. Figure 1.1 depicts the level of the Dow Jones Average during 1981. It appears to be characterized by typical short-term patterns. Yet when it is reconstructed in figure 1.2 as a chart of the weekly changes in the index, the symmetry disappears and is replaced by an apparently meaningless jumble.

The next two diagrams reverse the process. Figure 1.3 is a hypothetical series of random price changes. There neither is nor appears to be any pattern in figure 1.3. Yet when it is reconstructed in figure 1.4 as a chart of the levels of the counterfeit prices, the resulting graph acquires many of the characteristics of actual charts of the market, even to the "head and shoulders" pattern that is beloved by technical analysts.[1]

The moral of the story is this: Do not assume without questioning because there are regularities in price *levels* that

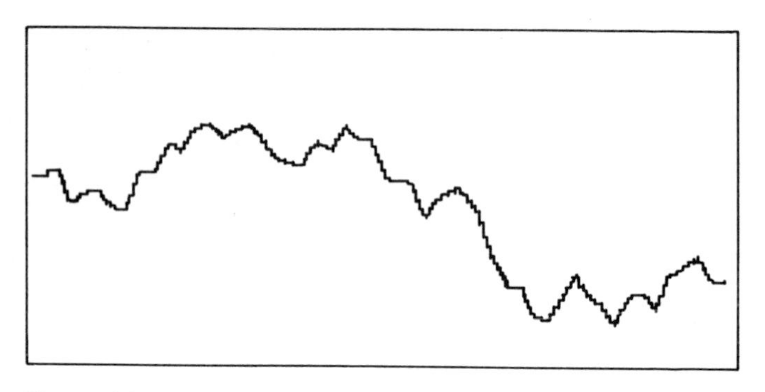

Figure 1.1
The weekly levels of the Dow Jones Average in 1981 appear to be characterized by regular patterns.

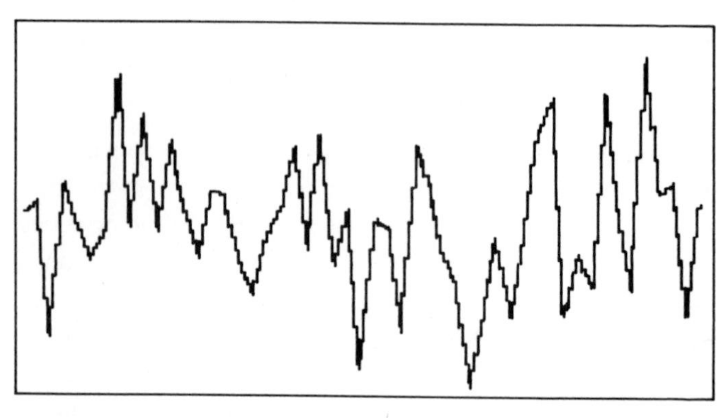

Figure 1.2
The changes in the Dow Jones do not appear to follow any pattern.

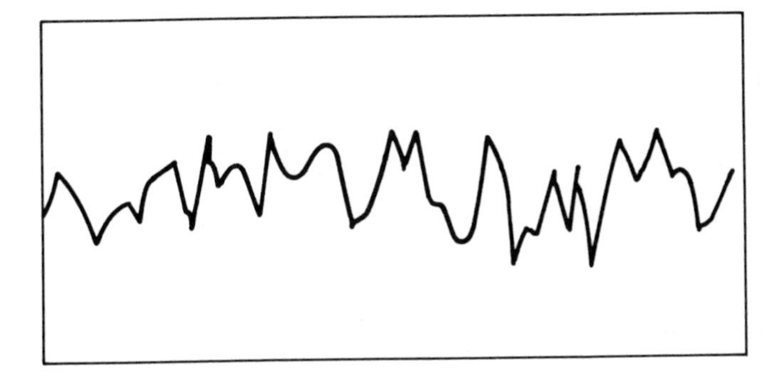

Figure 1.3
This series of random numbers looks like the changes in the Dow Jones Average.

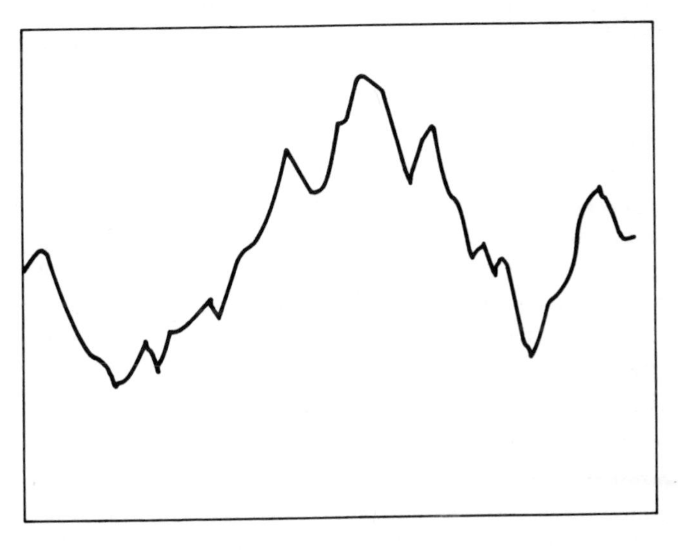

Figure 1.4
The cumulation of the series of random numbers looks like the level of the Dow Jones.

there must also be regularities in price *changes*. The charts that you have been studying may be no more than an accumulation of random price changes.

Some Statistical Tests of Price Patterns

As a simple check on this possibility, it is helpful to look at the extent to which price rises or falls tend to persist. In order to do this, we classify each price change as positive, zero, or negative and then count the runs of successive changes of the same sign. Thus the series + + + − 0 − would consist of four such runs. If there is a tendency for such changes to persist, the average length of run will be longer and the total number of runs will be less than if the same price changes were distributed randomly. A classic test of this kind examined the daily price changes of the thirty Dow Jones stocks over a period of about five years ending in 1962.[2] The first entry in table 1.1 shows the average actual number of runs for each stock. The second entry shows the average number of runs that we should expect if the plus days and minus days were mixed in a wholly random fashion. These figures suggest a very slight tendency for runs to persist, but it is negligible for most practical purposes. Indeed the remaining entries in table 1.1 show that when the exercise is repeated for four-, nine-, and sixteen-day changes, even this slight dependence disappears.

This simple runs test considered only the direction of price changes and took no account of their size. An alternative is to draw for each stock a scatter diagram like figure 1.5. The horizontal axis represents the daily change in the stock price, and the vertical axis represents the change on the following day. Each cross depicts the price movement of a hypothetical stock on a particular pair of days. If price changes are random, the crosses will be scattered incoherently over the chart as in figure 1.5. On the other hand, if the crosses tend to cluster along a straight line, we should have evidence of regularities in price behavior that might be worth exploiting.

Table 1.1
Actual and expected number of runs of consecutive price changes in the same direction for each of the Dow Jones stocks

	1-day change		4-day change		9-day change		16-day change	
	Actual	Expected	Actual	Expected	Actual	Expected	Actual	Expected
Average number of runs	735	760	176	176	75	75	42	42

Source: E. F. Fama, "The Behavior of Stock Market Prices," *Journal of Business* 38 (January 1965):34–105.

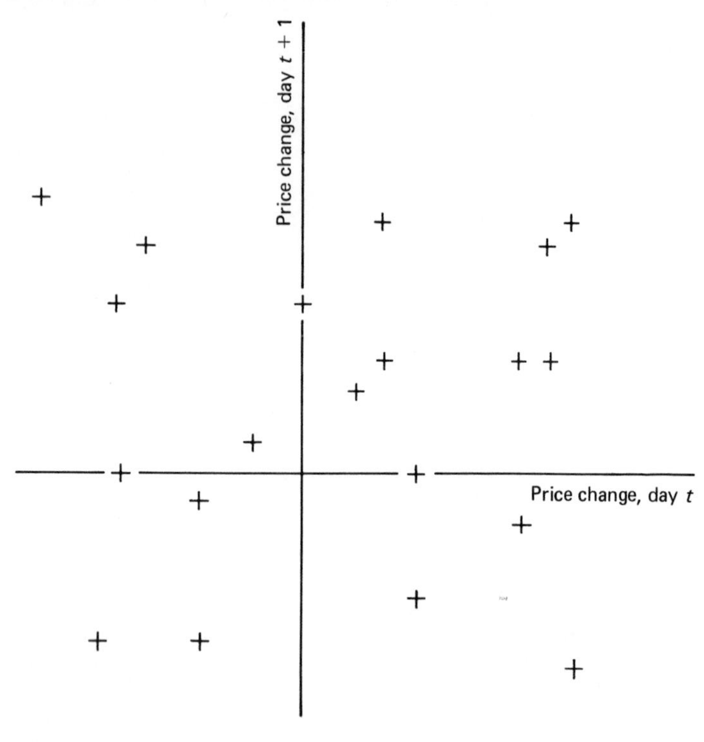

Figure 1.5
Each cross in this scatter diagram shows the price changes of a hypothetical stock in two successive periods.

Table 1.2
Average correlation between successive price changes for each of the Dow Jones stocks

	1-day changes	4-day changes	9-day changes	16-day changes
Correlation coefficient	0.03	−0.04	−0.05	0.01

Source: E. F. Fama, "The Behavior of Stock Market Prices," *Journal of Business* 38 (January 1965):34–105.

The correlation between successive price changes is a measure of the extent to which the crosses in our diagram tend to cluster along a straight line. The correlation may take any value between minus one and plus one. If there is no relationship between successive changes, the correlation will be zero. If each price change tends to be repeated, the correlation will be positive; if each change tends to be reversed, it will be negative.

Table 1.2 summarizes the correlation between the successive price changes of each of the Dow Jones stocks over the five years to 1962.[3] In each case the correlation is extremely close to zero, which is exactly what we should expect if price changes are random.

The runs test and the correlation analysis represent only a small sample of a vast number of such statistical studies of randomness in the price changes of common stocks. These studies have examined price changes over periods varying from a day to a month; they have extended back to 1875 and forward to the present day; they have looked for relationships between successive price changes and lagged price changes; they have covered stocks of both large and small firms. In no case was the random walk approximation seriously offended.

If you remain unconvinced that we are dealing with a fairly pervasive phenomenon, then look at table 1.3. It shows the correlation between successive monthly changes in the stock prices of thirty-six countries.[4] Technical analysts around the world seem to share a common affliction.

Two Common Technical Rules

These statistical analyses of price changes suggest that there are no worthwhile simple patterns in price fluctuations. But technical analysts could plead with some justification that statistical tests are not powerful enough to detect the complex relationships with which they are concerned. For example, suppose that there exists a group of professional investors who are better equipped than their fellows to assess a stock's worth. If their time is free and there are no costs to dealing, they will compete to buy or sell stock whenever the price differs from the estimated value. As a result, if the competition between professional investors is sufficiently intense, the stock price will never deviate from the estimated value.

In practice, the time of professional investors is not free and dealing costs are not zero. Therefore most investment managers are likely to require some minimum degree of misvaluation before they will act. In this case the stock price would be free to wander within limits. It would not fall below the estimated value by more than the professional investor's costs and it would not rise above the estimated value by more than those costs. Of course the professional investor's opinion of the stock's worth and, therefore, his buying and selling limits are also likely to change from time to time. In these circumstances prices would meander between periodically shifting barriers, as in figure 1.6.[5]

Notice that major price movements in figure 1.6 occur only when professionals change their expectations and adjust their buying and selling limits. Therefore, if investors really behave in this way, it might be profitable to use the following trading rule:

Table 1.3
Correlation between successive monthly changes of stock market indexes

Country	Correlation coefficient
Argentina	0.12
Australia	0.12
Austria	0.20
Belgium	−0.20
Brazil	0.08
Canada	−0.03
Ceylon	−0.15
Chile	0.05
Colombia	−0.11
Denmark	−0.23
Egypt	0.02
Finland	0.09
France	−0.19
Germany	0.17
Greece	0.25
Hong Kong	0.12
India	0.11
Ireland	0.40
Israel	−0.03
Italy	0.02
Japan	0.04
Lebanon	0.00
Mexico	0.00
Netherlands	0.01
New Zealand	−0.05
Norway	−0.24
Peru	−0.34
Philippines	0.01
Portugal	0.09
South Africa	0.11
Spain	−0.15

Table 1.3 (continued)

Country	Correlation coefficient
Sweden	−0.10
Switzerland	−0.09
United Kingdom	0.04
United States	−0.02
Venezuela	−0.11

Source: J. C. B. Cooper, "World Stock Markets: Some Random Walk Tests," *Applied Economics,* October 1982.

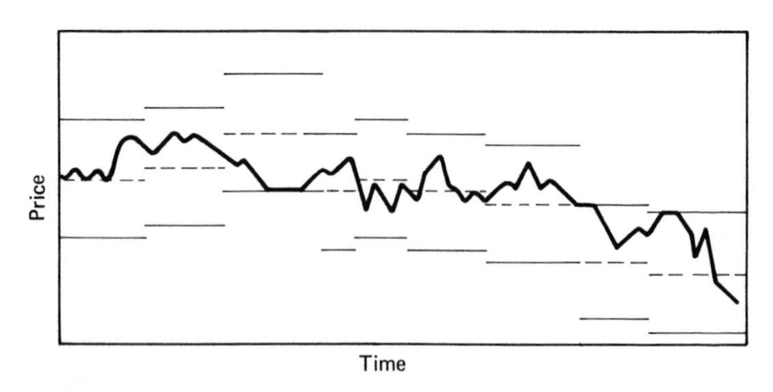

Figure 1.6
Hypothetical chart of a stock price that is free to wander within periodically changing limits.

Table 1.4
Average annual rates of return from filter rule, 1957–1962

Value of filter x	Return with trading strategy (%)	Total transactions with trading strategy	Return with trading strategy after commissions (%)
0.5	11.5	12,500	−103.6
1.0	5.5	8,700	− 74.9
2.0	0.2	4,800	− 45.2
4.0	0.1	2,000	− 19.5
6.0	1.3	1,100	− 9.4
8.0	1.7	700	− 5.0
10.0	3.0	400	− 1.4
20.0	4.3	100	3.0

Source: E. F. Fama and M. E. Blume, "Filter Rules and Stock Market Trading," *Journal of Business* 39 (January 1966):226–241.

If the daily closing price of a security rises at least x%, buy the security and hold it until its price moves down at least x% from a subsequent high. At that point sell the security short and maintain the short position until the price rises at least x% above a subsequent low.

By choosing a large value for the filter x, the investor would increase the probability that he is participating in a change in trend instead of merely a movement between barriers, but he would suffer the offsetting disadvantage of missing a large part of the move before he acted.

The first two columns of table 1.4 show the returns that you would have earned if you had used this filter rule to choose among the Dow Jones stocks during a five-year period.[6] Although the returns are positive, they are generally less than the 10 percent return you would have gotten if you had simply bought the Dow Jones stocks and left them alone. The remaining two columns of table 1.4 show both the number of transactions from following the filter strategy and the returns after dealing costs. They suggest that in each instance the only solace for the adherent of the filter rule would have been the gratitude of his broker.

The relative strength rule is another popular technical rule.[7] Its adherents also seek to exploit price trends, but they choose to concentrate on each stock's relative performance. Here is an example of the relative strength rule:

Each month measure the strength of the stock price by calculating the ratio of the current price to the average price over the previous six months. Start by investing equal amounts in the twenty stocks with the highest relative strength. Then continue to hold each of these stocks as long as they remain in the top 160 stocks in terms of relative strength. If any stock drops below this position, sell it and reinvest the proceeds in the current top twenty.

To assess the merit of such a rule, five separate eligible lists of 200 stocks each were selected from the stocks listed on the New York Stock Exchange (NYSE) in 1960.[8] From each of these eligible lists a portfolio was selected and managed according to the relative strength rule. The average return on these portfolios at the end of five years was compared with the return from buying and holding each of the stocks listed on the NYSE.

The results of this comparison and of similar comparisons for earlier five-year periods are shown in table 1.5. When dealing costs are ignored, the return from the relative strength rule was on average 0.8 percent a year higher than the return from the buy-and-hold strategy, but when one takes account of the costs of following the relative strength rule, the advantage is reversed.

In bull markets it is the risky stocks that generally have the highest returns; in bear markets it is the safest stocks. Therefore by following the relative strength rule an investor will tend to invest in risky stocks after a market rise and in

Table 1.5
Difference between returns from relative strength rule and buy-and-hold strategy

		Return (%)		
Period	Number of portfolios	Before costs	After costs	Risk-adjusted, after costs
1931–1935	3	−1.9	−3.7	−2.7
1936–1940	3	−3.5	−4.7	−5.6
1941–1945	4	−0.3	−2.3	−1.4
1946–1950	4	−0.5	−1.7	−1.7
1951–1955	5	2.7	1.5	0.2
1956–1960	5	7.8	6.8	5.7
1961–1965	5	1.4	0.1	−0.2
	Average	0.8	−0.6	−0.8

Source: M. C. Jensen, and G. A. Bennington, "Random Walks and Technical Theories: Some Additional Evidence," *Journal of Finance* 25 (May 1970):469–482

safe stocks after a market fall. More often than not the rule will produce portfolios with above-average risk. The final column of table 1.5 makes an adjustment for this difference in risk.[9] It shows that after dealing costs the risk-adjusted return from following the relative strength rule was on average 0.8 percent a year less than the risk-adjusted return from a simple buy-and-hold strategy.[10]

Stock Prices in a Well-Functioning Market

"October," Mark Twain observed, "is one of the peculiarly dangerous months to speculate in stocks in. The others are July, January, September, April, November, May, March, June, December, August and February." Although he was nearly right, there is some evidence that stocks perform better in January than in June. They also seem to perform better on Wednesday than Monday.[11] These are two examples of patterns that appear to exist, but you will not get rich on the basis of such patterns. The evidence is remarkably unanimous; for most practical purposes stock prices seem to follow a random walk.[12]

Early reaction to this finding was that it confirmed everybody's suspicion that investors are a whimsical and unpredictable bunch. Only later did economists come to realize that the result was exactly what we should expect in well-functioning securities markets.

In a free and competitive market, the stock price at each point in time depends on each investor's assessment of the security's true value. It, therefore, incorporates all the information available to investors. If a fresh piece of information subsequently becomes available, its implications will be examined and will cause a new price to be established. Because information is only new when it has not been deduced from earlier information, its effect on prices will be quite independent of anything that may have happened earlier. In other words, each price change will be unrelated to previous price changes.

Suppose, however, that a small number of investors do gain prior access to information. If that information is going to justify a rise in price, the knowledgeable individuals will be able to secure a profit by buying ahead of the market. Their purchases will cause the price to shift part way toward its new equilibrium. Subsequently, when the new information becomes publicly available, the price rise caused by the purchases of the experts will be followed by a further rise. Thus successive price changes will be related when there is a spreading awareness of information, and they will be unrelated when information is immediately and fully reflected in the stock price.

The existence of a limited number of experts with superior information will lead to dependence between successive prices. However, as long as the uninitiated are on their toes, such a situation cannot endure, for they will learn to spot what the experts are doing by examining past price changes and imitating the experts' behavior. If a sufficient number of buyers gain the advantage of the experts, the original situation is re-established. Each price change again becomes independent of the price changes that preceded it. Thus competition among fundamental analysts helps to ensure that information is rapidly discounted. And competition among technical analysts ensures that even if some investors do have superior information, their activities are rapidly discovered. In other words, both groups help keep stock price changes random.

Implications of the Random Walk Hypothesis

The term random has some unfortunate connotations. Random events are often believed to be in some sense "uncaused." This belief is partly due to misleading comparisons that are sometimes drawn between stock price changes and the behavior of a roulette wheel. The problem is liable to be translated into a philosophical one, but there is nothing mystical or unnatural about the process that generates stock price changes. It is not governed by some frolicsome gremlin. The random movement of stock prices simply results from competition between a large number of skilled and acquisitive investors.

A more specific misunderstanding is the view that the random walk hypothesis is inconsistent with a rising trend of stock prices. Regardless of whether the market is competitive, investors want a positive return for investing in risky securities. Moreover each of the tests that we have described has looked only at the sequence of price changes and has not been concerned with the average change.

It is sometimes suggested that the random character of stock price changes reflects unfavorably on the ability of the investment community. This is not true. The ease of entry into the industry and the high potential rewards presumably ensure the supply of at least some very able people. Beyond this, any useful conclusions are impossible, for whereas the notion of a perfect market implies a certain amount of equality among some of the protagonists, it is also consistent with wholly aimless investment by others.

It is even more difficult to draw any conclusions about the social value of investment activity. The competitive nature of the market might severely limit the extent to which some investors are able to profit at the expense of others, yet the community in general and investors indirectly still benefit in the form of efficiently distributed capital resources. In the same way, it may be meaningful to judge the value of an individual football team by the proportion of matches that it wins, but the value of football teams in general must be judged by some other criterion, such as the amount of enjoyment they provide.

Technical Analysis and Random Walks

Because the random character of stock price changes suggests that investment is a very competitive pastime, it has indirect implications for the fundamental analyst, which we shall consider in the next two chapters. Here we are concerned with the finding's direct challenge to the technical analyst. His activities may contribute to the maintenance of independence between successive price changes, but the existence of this independence removes all scope for profit by examination of the sequence of past price changes.

Although the evidence suggests that technical analysis is an unproductive pastime, it is impossible to prove that there are no relationships between successive price changes. It, therefore, remains possible that patterns exist for some stocks for some periods. Good managers, however, bet on probabilities, not possibilities. Given the evidence, it is difficult to justify setting out on a quest for the holy technical grail, and it is equally difficult to see how one could hope to be sure that any apparent regularity was not a passing coincidence.

If you are determined to embark on such a quest, it is important to be prepared for some of the snares that you may encounter. First, a number of apparently successful technical rules assume that information would have been available to the investor earlier than was in fact the case. One instance of this occurs when the sample from which the selection is to be made is both unrepresentative and unknown to the investor at the beginning of the period. For example, some years ago a senator gained considerable publicity with the claim that by throwing darts at the NYSE daily page of the Washington *Evening Star,* he had selected a portfolio that would have outperformed most mutual funds over the previous ten years. The senator had not considered that at the beginning of the period no investor would have had the benefit of knowing which stocks would have an NYSE quotation ten years later. Decision rules that assume the investor is aware of company earnings immediately after the end of the year suffer from a similar defect. In other cases, the trading rule is left vague. Certain apparent relationships between stock prices and other factors may be observed without any clear indication of how the relationship should be used or how to avoid signals that can be seen to be false only after the event.

Frequently the system is operable, but the profits are illusory and result from inadequate measures. For example, proponents of a particular technical rule often look only at capital gains and ignore differences in the dividend yield. On other occasions they may ignore the costs of switching from one stock to another. Or they may fail to recognize that the superior reward is needed to compensate for the additional risk. Just as common stocks are expected to offer higher returns than bonds, so stocks with above-average risk are expected to offer higher returns than those with below-average risk.

With a little care it is possible to detect the systems that would never even have been successful in the past. However, the fact that a trading rule would have been profitable in the past is no guarantee that it will continue to be so in the future. If you examine a sufficient number of possible rules, you can be certain that eventually you will find one that would have been profitable over a particular past period, but this success may be no more than a coincidence. Repeated analysis of the same body of data is often known as data mining. It is unlike any other kind of mining, for the resource is never depleted, but all that you extract is fool's gold. If you must data mine, put aside some data from a different period to check whether the apparent patterns that you discover in the first sample really do persist.

It is a costly and tedious business to check the profitability of technical rules. But it is likely to be even more costly to use such a rule without first assessing its value. If the rule does not work, you will make unnecessary transactions and your portfolio will be poorly diversified. Faced with this unenviable choice, the wise investment manager ignores the siren song of the technical analyst.

Notes

1. This visual comparison was first suggested by Roberts (5).

2. See Fama (4).

3. See Fama (4).

4. See Cooper (1). Indexes of stocks that are infrequently traded may exhibit spurious patterns (see Working (7)). Despite this, the general impression in table 1.3 is that there is very little relationship between successive market movements.

5. The possibility of these barriers was suggested in Cootner (3).

6. See Fama and Blume (10).

7. The principal advocate of the relative strength rule is Levy (13, 14).

8. The tests described here are by Jensen and Bennington (12).

9. More precisely, it shows the difference between the return from following the relative strength rule and the return from holding an equally volatile package of risk-free loans and the market index. The rationale for such a measure is discussed in chapter 10.

10. Obviously there are countless variations on this relative strength rule. Jensen and Bennington also analyzed the results from buying ten rather than twenty stocks. The performance of these ten-stock portfolios was somewhat worse than that of the twenty-stock portfolios.

11. See references listed at the end of this chapter.

12. An excellent collection of the earlier studies on the random walk hypothesis is that of Cootner (2).

References

Some statistical tests of the random walk:

(1) Cooper, J. C. B. "World Stockmarkets: Some Random Walk Tests." *Applied Economics,* October 1982.

(2) Cootner, P. H., ed. *The Random Character of Stock Market Prices.* Cambridge, Mass.: The MIT Press, 1964.

(3) Cootner, P. H. "Stock Prices: Random Walks vs. Finite Markov Chains." *Industrial Management Review* 3 (Spring 1962):24–45. Reprinted under the title "Stock Prices: Random vs. Systematic Changes," in Cootner, ed. *The Random Character of Stock Market Prices.*

(4) Fama, E. F. "The Behavior of Stock Market Prices." *Journal of Business* 38 (January 1965):34–105.

(5) Roberts, H. V. "Stock Market 'Patterns' and Financial Analysis: Methodological Suggestions." *Journal of Finance* 14 (March 1959):1–10. Reprinted in Cootner, ed., *The Random Character of Stock Market Prices.*

(6) Solnik, B. "A Note on the Validity of the Random Walk for European Stock Prices." *Journal of Finance* 28 (December 1973):1151–1159.

(7) Working, H. "Note on the Correlation of First Differences of Averages in a Random Chain." *Econometrica* 28 (October 1960):916–918. Reprinted in Cootner, ed., *The Random Character of Stock Market Prices.*

Some tests of simple trading rules:

(8) Alexander, S. S. "Price Movements in Speculative Markets: Trends or Random Walks." *Industrial Management Review* 2 (May 1961):7–26. Reprinted in Cootner, ed., *The Random Character of Stock Market Prices.*

(9) Alexander, S. S. "Price Movements in Speculative Markets: Trends or Random Walks, Number 2." *Industrial Management Review* 5 (Spring 1964):25–46. Reprinted in Cootner, ed., *The Random Character of Stock Market Prices.*

(10) Fama, E. F., and Blume, M. E. "Filter Rules and Stock Market Trading." *Journal of Business* 39 (January 1966):226–241.

(11) James, F. E., Jr. "Monthly Moving Averages—An Effective Investment Tool?" *Journal of Financial and Quantitative Analysis* 3 (September 1968):315–326.

(12) Jensen, M. C., and Bennington, G. A. "Random Walks and Technical Theories: Some Additional Evidence." *Journal of Finance* 25 (May 1970):469–482.

(13) Levy, R. A. "Random Walks: Reality or Myth." *Financial Analysts Journal* 23 (November–December 1967):69–77.

(14) Levy, R. A. "Relative Strength as a Criterion for Investment Selection." *Journal of Finance* 22 (December 1967):595–610.

These studies of weekly and monthly patterns are interesting exceptions to the random walk theory:

(15) Bonin, J. M., and Moses, E. A. "Seasonal Variation in Prices of Individual Dow Jones Industrial Stocks." *Journal of Financial and Quantitative Analysis* 9 (December 1974):963–991.

(16) Cross, F. "The Behavior of Stock Prices on Fridays and Mondays." *Financial Analysts Journal* 29 (November–December 1973):2–69.

(17) French, K. R. "Stock Returns and the Weekend Effect." *Journal of Financial Economics* 8 (March 1980): 55–70.

(18)Gibbons, M. R., and Hess, P. J. "Day of the Week Effects and Asset Returns." *Journal of Business* 54 (1981):579–596.

(19) Rozeff, M. S., and Kinney, W. R., Jr. "Capital Market Seasonality: The Case of Stock Returns." *Journal of Financial Economics* 3 (1976):379–402.

Samuelson's paper shows that in an efficient market, prices move randomly:

(20) Samuelson, P. A. "Proof that Properly Anticipated Prices Fluctuate Randomly." *Industrial Management Review* 6 (Spring 1965):41–49.

2 Fundamental Analysis and Publicly Available Information

The evidence that stock prices follow a random walk is a direct challenge to the technical analyst, who believes that the study of past price changes can help to forecast future price changes. It is also an indirect challenge to the fundamental analyst, who believes that a study of the company's business can help to forecast future stock prices. If it is indeed true that stock prices already reflect all available information about the company, then the fundamental analyst will be unable to make superior profits.

A market in which prices reflect available information is known as an efficient market. The random walk evidence showed that stock prices at least reflect the information that is available in past stock prices. So the market is efficient in this weak sense. In this chapter we shall consider whether stock prices also reflect other kinds of publicly available information. That would be evidence of a stronger form of efficiency.[1]

Since it is impossible to examine every item of news that should have affected the stock price, we shall concentrate on the market's reaction to four different events: the dividend announcement, the publication of money supply figures, the announcement of stock splits, and the occurrence of a block trade.

Stock Prices and Dividend Announcements

A stock's worth depends on what investors expect to get out of it; in other words, it depends on the expected future stream of dividends. The company's dividend announcement therefore represents an important and relevant item of information. Depending on whether the dividend is higher or lower than expected, the stock is likely to perform better or worse than average. If the market is efficient, this price adjustment will occur as soon as the dividend is announced; if it is not efficient, then the adjustment will not be immediate, and the quick-witted investor will be able to make superior profits.

In order to isolate the effect of the new information on the stock price, it is helpful to adjust for changes in the general market level. To do this we can estimate how much the stock price would normally have changed given the movement in the market and then calculate the difference between the stock's actual price change and its "normal" change.

Figure 2.1 shows the abnormal daily price behavior of 135 NYSE stocks around the dividend announcement date.[2] Notice first that dividend changes are indeed important. Firms announcing substantial dividend increases have above-average performance and those announcing unchanged or reduced dividends have below-average performance.

Depending on whether the dividend announcement occurred before or after the market close, the market's first opportunity to react to the news was on day 0 or day 1. Therefore, in an efficient market the effect of the announcement should be impounded in the stock price by day 1. This is exactly what figure 2.1 shows. There were quite sharp price adjustments on days 0 and 1, but it would have been impossible to earn superior profits by buying or selling after that time.

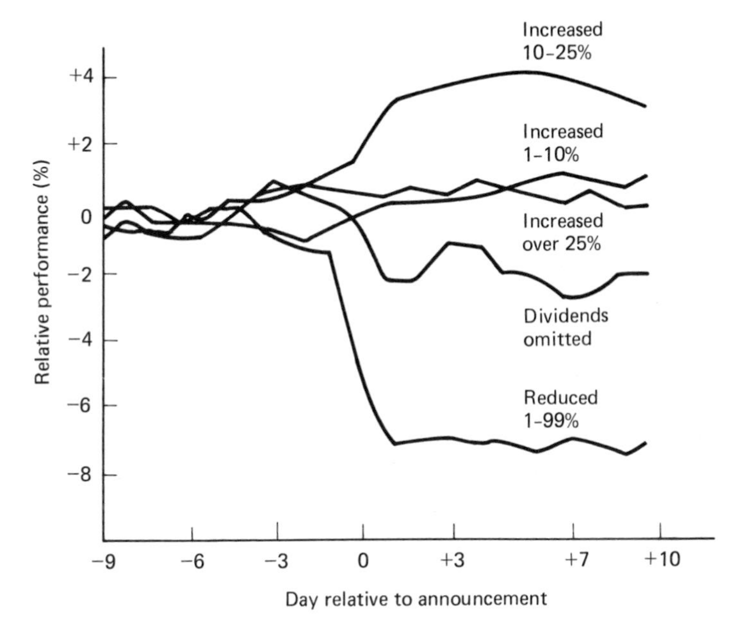

Figure 2.1
Relative performance of stocks during the days surrounding a dividend announcement. From R. R. Pettit, "Dividend Announcements, Security Performance and Capital Market Efficiency," *Journal of Finance* 27 (December 1972):993–1007.

As a check on this finding, it is worth looking at the longer-term reaction to dividend announcements and at the same time enlarging the sample to include 18,000 announcements between 1964 and 1968. Figure 2.2 shows the abnormal monthly changes in the stock price on either side of the announcement date. Although the abnormal price movements before the announcement month suggest that the market often had some forewarning of the forthcoming dividend, the largest single price change occurred during the announcement month itself. If the market is efficient, the investor should not expect to be able to make superior profits by buying or selling after the announcement month. In general that was so, but there were two curious anomalies. In the case of dividend omissions the price continued to drift down after the announcement month, and in the case of initial payments it continued to drift up. We cannot be sure whether this is an indication of inefficiency or a result of the manner in which the sample was selected or simply a coincidence.

Stock Prices and the Money Supply

Despite the apparent anomalies, the generally rapid response of the market to the dividend announcement suggests that there is little opportunity to make superior profits solely with the aid of the more obvious kinds of public information. Nevertheless, it remains possible that the market cannot immediately evaluate rather more subtle items of news. For example, it is often argued that an unexpected change in the money supply causes investors to adjust their portfolios by exchanging money for common stock and other assets. If this response is not instantaneous, then there may be an opportunity for the more agile investor to take advantage of the lag to make abnormal profits.

Figure 2.3 illustrates some early evidence that changes in monetary policy herald changes in the level of stock prices. From 1918 to 1963 there was an apparent tendency for a reduction in the rate of growth in money supply to precede declining stock prices by about fifteen months and for an increase in the rate of growth to precede rising prices by about two months.[3] On the surface figure 2.3 suggests that investors are passing up profitable opportunities, but as we know, visual impressions can be misleading. Some harder evidence is required before telephoning your stockbroker.

There is considerable evidence that stock prices and monetary policy are related. For example, 15 percent of the var-

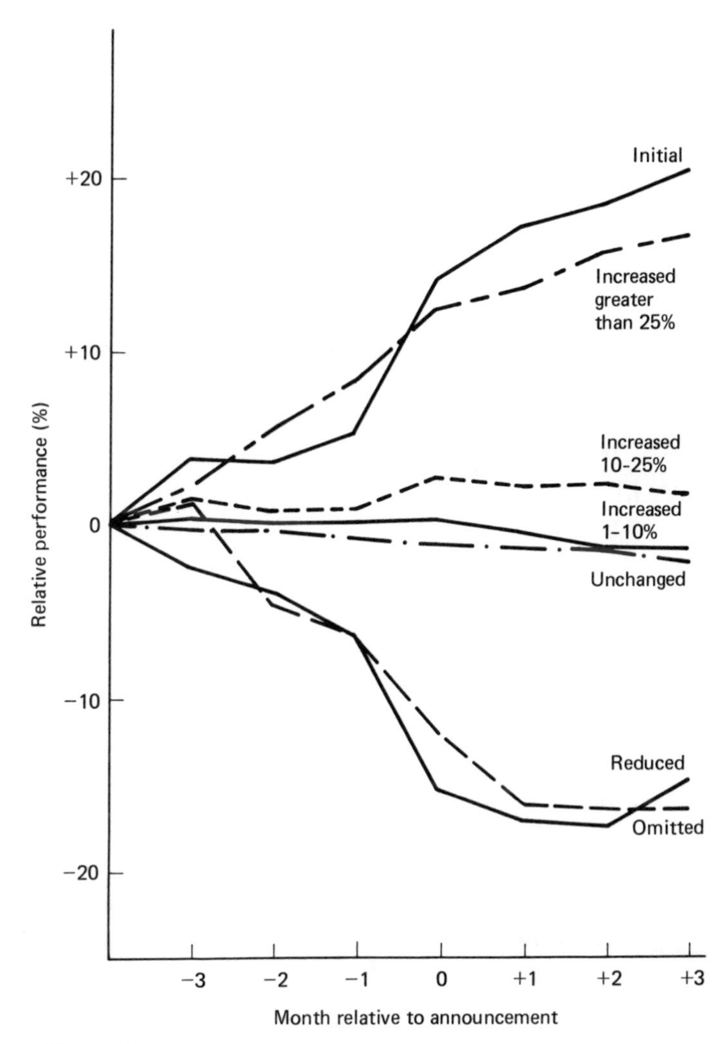

Figure 2.2
Relative performance of stocks during the months surrounding a dividend announcement. From R. R. Pettit, "Dividend Announcements, Security Performance and Capital Market Efficiency," *Journal of Finance* 27 (December 1972):993–1007.

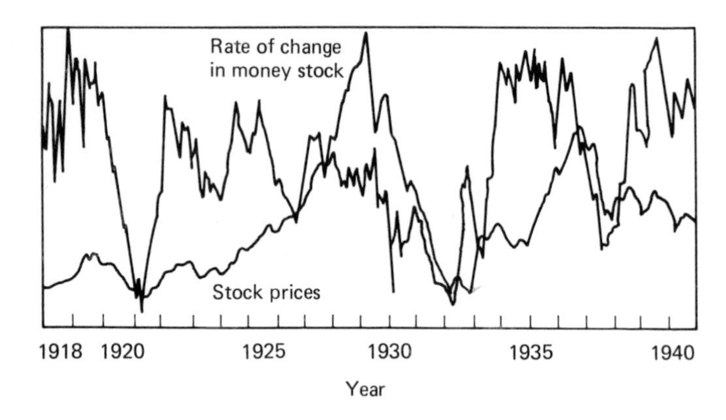

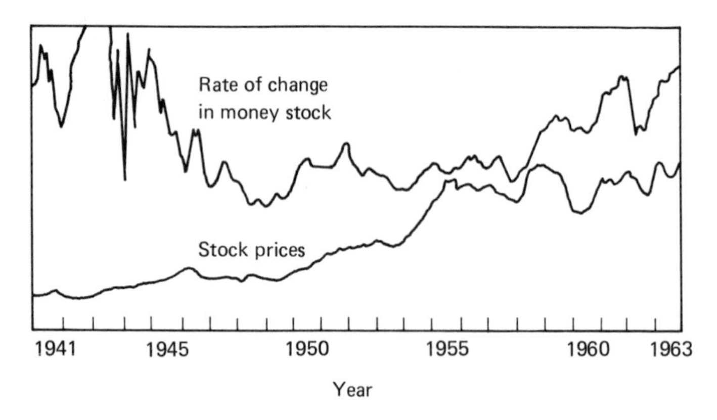

Figure 2.3
Variations in the growth rate of the money supply seem to have anticipated changes in stock prices. From B. W. Sprinkel, *Money and Stock Prices*(Homewood, Ill.: Richard D. Irwin, 1964).

iation in monthly market returns between 1948 and 1970 could be explained in terms of the variations in the monthly rates of growth in the money supply during the preceding seventeen months and the subsequent eight months.[4] In other words, an investor could potentially have made superior market forecasts if he knew past rates of growth in the money supply and could forecast future rates of growth.

Although this result confirms the existence of a relationship between stock prices and money supply, it does not tell us whether the relationship was leading or lagging. If we look only at changes in the money supply during the earlier months, the proportion of the variation in monthly market returns that could be explained in terms of past variations in the money supply falls to 10 percent.

This link between market return and prior money supply growth is not strong, but it does seem to indicate that the market does not take account of all available information. However, there are two things that we have forgotten. First, money supply figures are published only with a delay, so at the beginning of the month the investor would not have known the money supply growth in the preceding month. Second, the figures are initially published in preliminary form and are frequently subject to revision. Therefore, to assess how well an investor could in fact have forecast market returns from publicly available information, the exercise was repeated again using only unrevised money supply data available at the beginning of the month. In this case, the variation in the growth of the money supply could explain only 2 percent of the variation in monthly stock returns.

This very weak relationship suggests that market prices largely reflect published money supply data, so there is little opportunity for an investor to earn superior profits from such information. For example, suppose that each month from October 1956 to November 1970 an investor employed the following rule:

First, use post-1947 data to estimate the relationship between published changes in the money supply growth and the subsequent market return. Then use this relationship to predict the market return for the coming month. If the predicted market return is higher than the rate of interest, invest in common stocks; otherwise invest in short-term loans.

By following such a rule our investor would have earned an average monthly return of 0.68 percent before transaction costs. However, he could have earned an average monthly return of 0.71 percent simply by investing an equivalent constant proportion of his money in stocks and short-term loans.

These results confirm the statistical analysis. Although there is a measurable relationship between money supply and stock prices, this is of little use unless you can forecast the money supply better than your fellows. You cannot earn superior profits if you know only the published figures. These are already reflected in market prices.

Stock Prices and Stock Splits

Stock splits and stock dividends change neither the real assets of the corporation nor the division of ownership. For a large concern, the expenses involved can amount to several hundred thousand dollars. Yet there is a common belief that they confer substantive benefits on the stockholder that are reflected in the price of the security. For example, the chairman of Rohr Aircraft once rallied his stockholders with the assurance that the stock dividend would offer them "a greater return while at the same time conserving cash to finance the company's anticipated growth." Similarly, the president of Mohasco observed that the stock dividend would "provide shareholders with tangible evidence of the proposed investment by issuing additional shares to them and by placing this investment on a dividend paying basis."[5] If these managers are right, the announcement of a split or stock dividend should prompt a rise in the stock price.

One classic study examined the market's reaction to 940 stock splits.[6] In each instance at least five shares were distributed for every four previously outstanding, and the sample covered substantially all the distributions of this size occurring on the New York Stock Exchange between 1927 and 1959.

Figure 2.4 shows the average performance of the 940 stocks after adjusting for changes in the general level of the market. In other words, it depicts the relative performance of a portfolio of stocks, each of which was acquired thirty months before the occurrence of a split. For much of this time investors could not have been aware of the impending split, so the split could not have been responsible for the unusual appreciation that characterized the initial months. It seems, therefore, that directly or indirectly stock splits must be a consequence of rising stock prices.

This abnormal appreciation accelerated sharply in the-month of the split, but at that point it ceased.[7] Though individual securities may have continued to rise relative to the market, there was no general price trend after the split occurred. Indeed at no time during the next two and a half years did the prices vary by as much as 1 percent from the level at the time of the split.

At first sight this result is odd, for the firms continued to experience unusual prosperity. For example, over two-thirds of the companies increased their dividends by an above-average amount in the year following the split. As we saw earlier in the chapter, this would normally produce a significant rise in price, but in the case of the split stocks it looks as if the dividend increase caused no surprise. This can only be because the announcement of the split was accompanied by an explicit promise of higher dividends or because it was interpreted by the market as foreshadowing

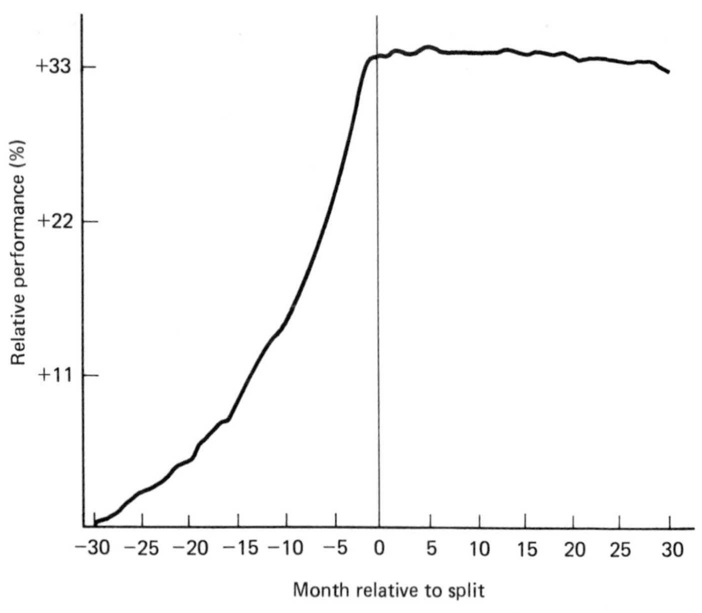

Figure 2.4
Relative performance of 940 stocks over the period of a split. From E. F. Fama, L. Fisher, M. C. Jensen, and R. Roll, "The Adjustment of Stock Prices to New Information," *International Economic Review* 10 (February 1969):1–21.

such good news. If this is so, the appreciation that accompanies the split may have nothing to do with a taste for splits as such but may simply stem from the fact that the company's action is regarded as a gesture of confidence in the future.

Figure 2.5 isolates the price movement of those stocks that provided an above-average increase in dividends. Notice that before the split they appreciated more rapidly than the entire group. Several things may have caused investors to be more confident about these stocks, but the significant point about this behavior is that it supports the view that the price movement at the time of the split is a consequence only of the extent to which investors are led to revise their assessment of the firm's prospects.

Figure 2.6 also accords well with this notion. It portrays the price movement of the smaller number of stocks for which no relative increase in dividends was forthcoming. The fact that these issues rose at all in the presplit months is a sign that at the time investors could not always identify them. Over the following year, however, as the market came to realize that its hopes were misplaced, these stocks fell back in price until they stood at the same level as they were five months before the split.

Thus, investors do not appear to be fooled into believing that a stock split gives them something for nothing. But they do seem to be aware that a split is generally an indication of company prosperity, and it is this that causes the stock price to rise at the time of the split. Not only does the rise in price reflect accurately the odds of an increased dividend payment, but the implications of the split are impounded in the stock price by the end of the split month. Therefore, it is impossible to profit from knowledge of the split after it has taken place.

Stock Prices and Secondary Distributions

If a substantial price reduction is needed to sell more of an article, demand is said to be inelastic. Normally, this is the case when no close substitute is readily available. For example, as long as there is only one *Mona Lisa*, art collectors are prepared to pay a very high price for it, but if a dozen *Mona Lisa*s appeared on the market, you could be confident that the price would fall sharply.

Many fund managers seem to think that a company's common stock is rather like the *Mona Lisa* and that they cannot sell more than a small proportion of their holding without severely depressing the price.

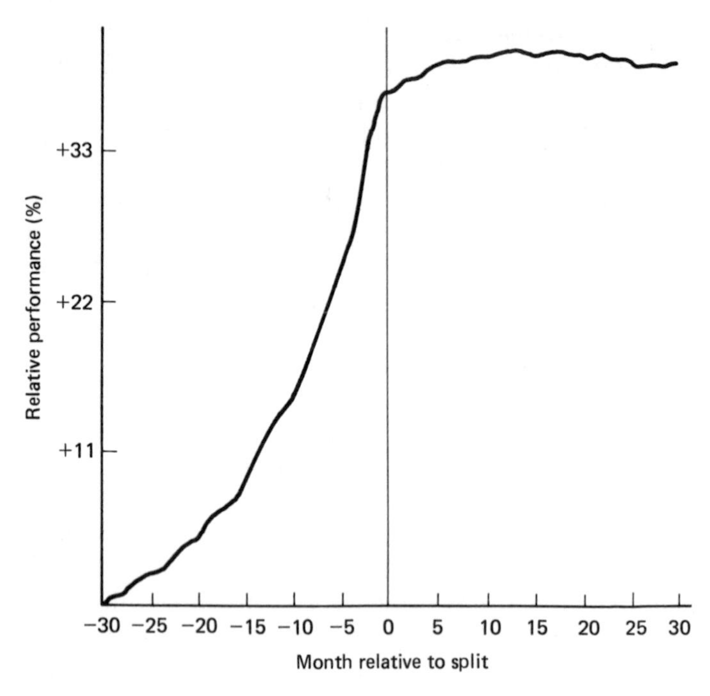

Figure 2.5
Relative performance of stocks for which a split was succeeded by a relative increase in dividend. From E. F. Fama et al., "The Adjustment of Stock Prices to New Information," *International Economic Review* 10 (February 1969):1–21.

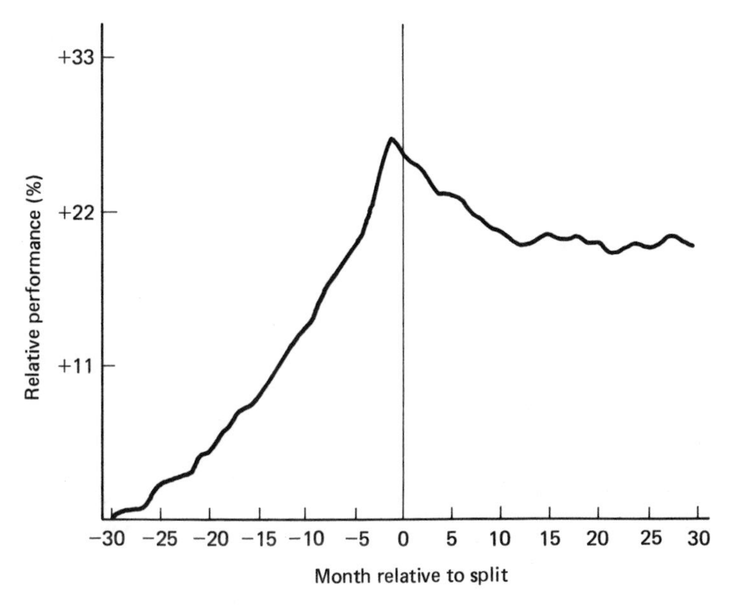

Figure 2.6
Relative performance of stocks for which a split was not succeeded by a relative increase in dividend. From E. F. Fama et al., "The Adjustment of Stock Prices to New Information," *International Economic Review* 10 (February 1969):1–21.

The strange thing about this view is that the stock of a single company is not generally prized for its unique qualities. Some investors may own Xerox for sentimental reasons, but most own the stock because it offers the prospect of a return that is adequate compensation for the risks involved. Since every other stock is held for a similar reason, only a small relative decline in the price of Xerox should be required to bring in many buyers who previously felt that it was no more attractive than other securities. In that case, an increase in the supply of stock should not have a significant effect on the price unless it is large relative to the supply of all available stocks. The situation would be like that of a wheat farmer. Since his wheat is no different from that of other farmers, he can sell additional quantities with only an imperceptible effect on the price.

One way to investigate the ability of the market to digest large offers of stock is to examine its reaction to secondary distributions. These are sales of large quantities of stock that cannot easily be disposed of in the regular manner on the New York Stock Exchange and that are, therefore, sold off the floor of the exchange.

Figure 2.7 shows the abnormal price movement of 1,200 stocks during the months surrounding a secondary distribution.[8] It is clear that the distribution is typically associated with a modest fall in price. Most of this fall occurs in the month of the distribution, when there was an average decline of just over 2 percent. During the following eighteen months the price drifted further downward by 1.5 percent. Figure 2.8 provides a more detailed picture of the performance of 345 stocks during the days surrounding the distribution. Over the entire forty-day period the stocks suffered a decline of 2.3 percent, the major part of which occurred on the day of sale and the five following days.

Although the price fall is rather less than is commonly supposed, there does seem to be some basis for the fund manager's complaint that it is difficult to sell large quantities of stock without depressing the price. However, if the decline was just a matter of market indigestion, one might expect a recovery when the digestive processes were complete. The analysis of daily data shows no trace of such a recovery, and the monthly figures show only a very limited rally.[9]

The fact that the secondary distribution coincided with a permanent reduction in price suggests that this decline was not simply a consequence of the additional supply of stock. Figure 2.9 provides some further evidence on the matter. Each point in this scatter diagram shows the size of a sec-

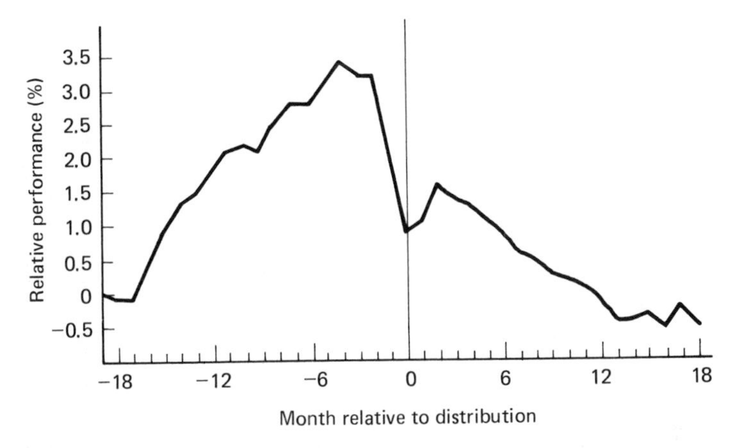

Figure 2.7
Relative performance of 1,200 stocks in the months surrounding a secondary distribution. From M. Scholes, "The Market for Securities: Substitution versus Price Pressure and the Effects of Information on Share Prices," *Journal of Business* 45 (April 1972):179–211.

ondary distribution and the decline in price on the day of the offer. It is clear that the decline was no greater when $100 million of stock was sold than when the figure was $100,000. It could be argued that the size of the offer should have been measured in terms of the proportion of the firm's stock that was involved. The analysis was therefore repeated with this modification. It made no difference: the price decline was no greater when 30 percent of the firm's stock was sold than when the proportion was less than 0.1 percent.[10]

If it cost no more to shift $100 million of stock than $100,000, demand must be very elastic. Why then does the price fall at the time of a secondary distribution? There is one plausible explanation. The secondary distribution could be associated with a permanent downward shift in demand for the stock. This would occur if the distribution coincided with the publication of bad news or if investors interpreted

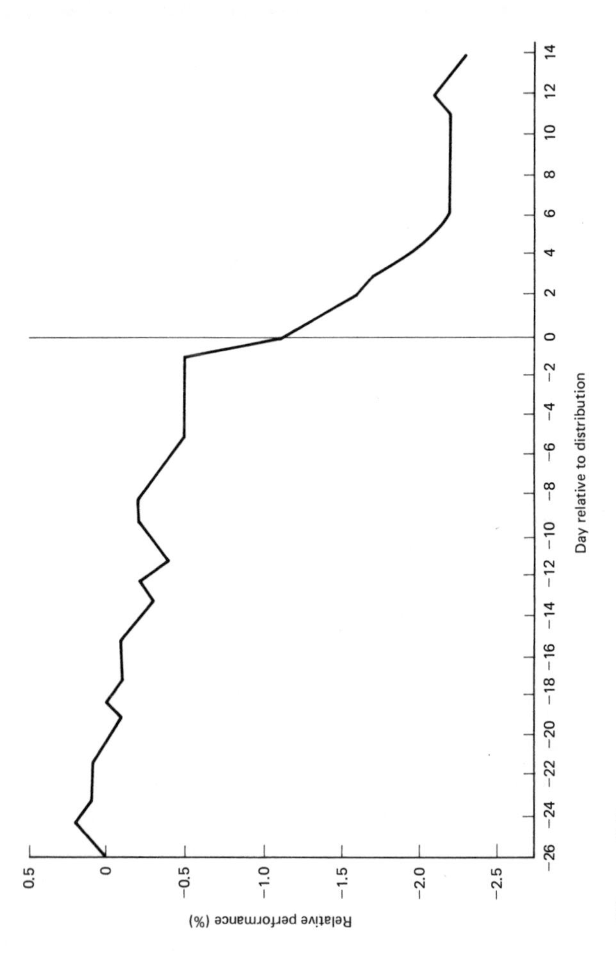

Figure 2.8
Relative performance of 345 stocks during days surrounding a secondary distribution. From M. Scholes, "The Market for Securities: Substitution versus Price Pressure and the Effects of Information on Share Prices," *Journal of Business* 45 (April 1972):179–211.

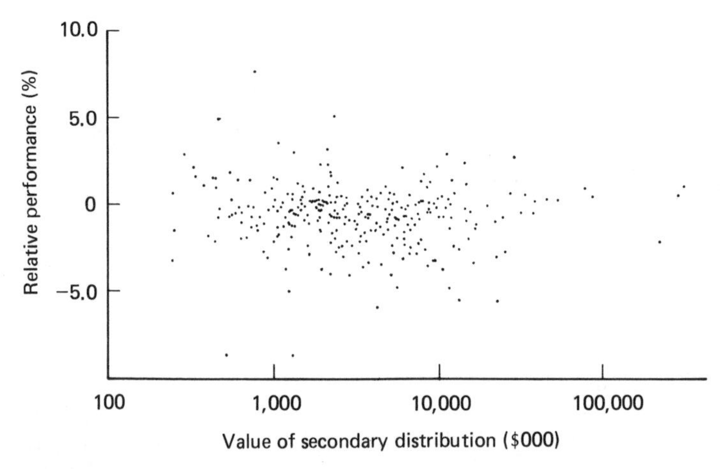

Figure 2.9
Each point on the scatter diagram shows the size of the secondary distribution and the price change on the day of offer. From M. Scholes, "The Market for Securities: Substitution versus Price Pressure and the Effects of Information on Share Prices," *Journal of Business* 45 (April 1972):179–211.

the offering as the harbinger of such news and so revised downward their assessment of the stock's value. The fact that the price never recovered from its new level would fully justify such a reaction.

It is instructive to consider in this light the market's response to different kinds of secondary distribution. Some are registered with the Securities and Exchange Commission, and a twenty-day waiting period is then enforced before the sale can take place. Since the owner is unlikely to register an issue if he is in possession of private information, registered distributions should prompt an earlier but smaller decline in price. Figure 2.10 confirms that this is exactly what happens.

Figure 2.11 shows the performance of the stocks according to the type of seller. Notice that during the month of dis-

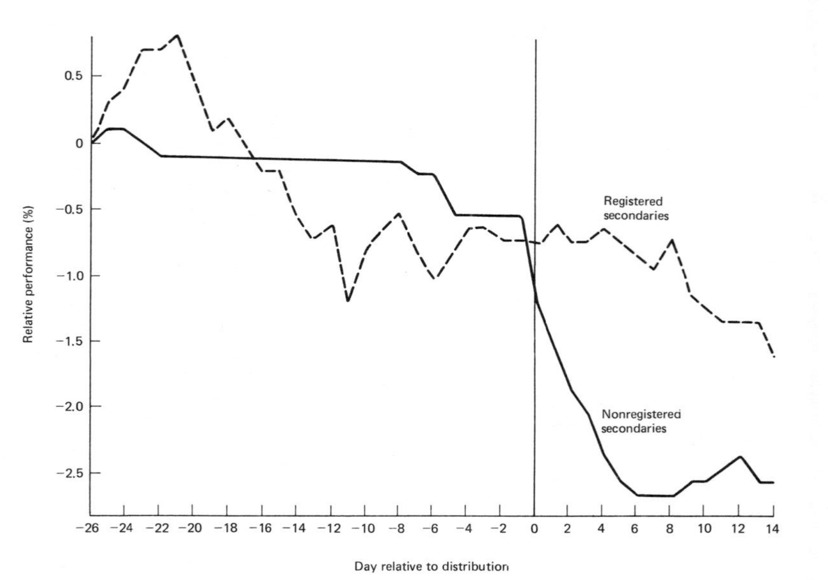

Figure 2.10
The effect on prices of registered and unregistered secondary distributions. From M. Scholes, "The Market for Securities: Substitution versus Price Pressure and the Effects of Information on Share Prices," *Journal of Business* 45 (April 1972):179–211.

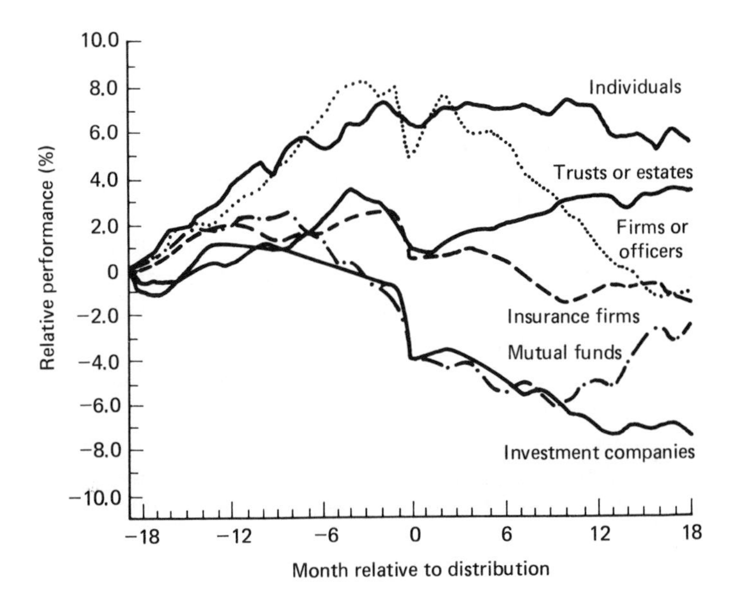

Figure 2.11
Relative performance over the period of a secondary distribution according to the type of seller. From M. Scholes, "The Market for Securities: Substitution versus Price Pressure and the Effects of Information on Share Prices," *Journal of Business* 45 (April 1972):179–211.

tribution, the decline was most severe when the stock was sold by a company officer, investment company, or mutual fund. In contrast, the decline was least marked when the seller was an individual or trust company. This distinction applies not only to the month but to the day of sale. This is somewhat surprising, since in the case of unregistered distributions the identity of the seller is not disclosed until later. At least two explanations are possible. It may be that company officers, investment companies, and mutual funds are more prone to sell large amounts of stock as soon as unfavorable news appears. It is also likely that investors often guess the identity of the seller and then react according to the amount of information they believe him to possess. It seems plausible to suppose that individuals and trusts often sell stock to satisfy a need for cash, so block offerings by these groups should cause little concern. Corporate officers, on the other hand, are always likely to be well informed, so any indication that an insider was selling stock would understandably create some alarm. If the market did in fact reason in this way, it was in retrospect fully justified. Figure 2.11 demonstrates that on average the stocks sold by individuals and trusts did not perform unusually badly. At the other extreme, offerings by insiders were followed by a more substantial decline in price.[11] The performance of stocks sold by other institutions was less decisive, but in each instance the offering typically preceded some months of relatively poor price performance.

Stock Prices, Public Information, and Fundamental Analysis

In this chapter we have considered the market's reaction to four kinds of public information. The first study focused on the company's dividend announcement. Since the value of a stock depends directly on the cash that it produces, it is not surprising that the stock price reacts rapidly to news of the dividend.

Our second study was concerned with stock prices and the money supply. Although we might expect variations in the money supply to affect stock prices, the relationship is more subtle than it is for dividends. The fact that the market seems able to identify and evaluate such indirect items of information is somewhat more of a threat to the fundamental analyst and must limit his opportunities to make superior profits.

In our third example, we widened the definition of public information to include signals by management or well-informed investors. Some signals, such as a chairman's annual statement or a broker's report, are overt expressions of opinion, but in other cases the signal may be no more than a nod or a wink. The stock split is rather like a wink; it does not affect the company's value, but it does indicate management's confidence in the future. The market is aware of this, and the stock price moves accordingly.

Not all signals are voluntary. Whenever an investor buys or sells a large block of stock, he alerts others to the possibility that he may know something that they do not. As a result even superior investment judgment may be worthless unless it can be hidden. This is the principal message of the study of secondary distributions. The message is familiar to security dealers. They cannot stay in business if the stocks that they hold consistently earn a below-average rate of return. So when they set their buying and selling prices, they try to ensure that on average they will earn at least a fair return and that the investors who deal with them will not profit at their expense. As a result you can beat the market only if you know more than the other investors who are buying and selling.[12] To make matters worse, uninformed investors will try to demonstrate their ignorance to the dealer. If they succeed, he will quote a better price to them and a worse price to the remainder. In this case you will beat the market only if you know more than the other well-informed investors who are buying and selling.

The studies described in this chapter were selected because they considered the market's response to four very different types of publicly available information. They are not, however, the only items of information that have been analyzed. Other studies have examined the market's reaction to earnings announcements, stock repurchases, rights issues, exchange listings, changes in accounting methods, mergers, tender offers, and stockbrokers' recommendations.[13] Some of these events have a direct bearing on the value of the stock; others are important because they provide signals of other people's views. In each case, the predominant impression is that the stock price responds quickly and efficiently to the news. Once the information has become public, there is little opportunity to make superior profits.

Of course, it would be surprising if the evidence was unanimous. For example, we have already seen that there appears to have been some delay in the market's reaction to the announcement of a dividend omission or an initial dividend payment. Researchers have also become increasingly aware of the difficulties involved in measuring accurately the market's reaction to new information. But, while the empirical evidence may be somewhat less conclusive than it once seemed, it remains unlikely that in such competitive conditions you could expect to make superior profits solely with the aid of public information. Even if we cannot be sure that some kinds of information are impounded quickly and accurately in the stock price, it would be difficult to identify continuing profit opportunities with any degree of confidence. The only sensible basis for an investment policy is to assume that you need some superior information to make consistently superior profits.

Notes

1. For a somewhat more technical discussion of the meaning of efficiency and of the empirical evidence, see Fama (55).

2. Our description of the market's reaction to dividend announcements is taken from Pettit (2). A similar study is described in Charest (1).

3. This suggestion that money supply figures are a leading indicator of stock price changes is taken from Sprinkel (12).

4. This description is taken from Rozeff (11).

5. These two examples were cited in Walter (21).

6. This study of stock splits is described in Fama, Fisher, Jensen, and Roll (17).

7. For some curious, more recent evidence that the market's reaction to the announcement of the split is not instantaneous, see Charest (16).

8. This description of the effect of secondary distributions is taken from Scholes (27).

9. In a study of block trades, Kraus and Stoll (25) found evidence of very slight price pressure. For example, a block sale initially depressed the stock price by 1.9 percent, but by the end of the day, the price had recovered 0.7 percent from this level. A study of block trades by Dann et al. (23) suggested that the price recovery was completed within fifteen minutes.

10. In a study of U.K. rights issues, Marsh (26) also found no relationship between the amount of stock on offer and the behavior of the stock price.

11. The references at the end of this chapter cite some other evidence that insiders do indeed make superior investment profits.

12. A dealer is always likely to lose by trading with a well-informed investor. Therefore, the dealer will set his prices so that his losses to well-informed investors are at least offset by the profits he makes from the uninformed investor. This point was first made by Treynor, writing under the pseudonym of Bagehot (54).

13. A sample of these studies is listed in the references to this chapter.

References

Some studies of the market reaction to dividend announcements:

(1) Charest, G. "Dividend Information, Stock Returns and Market Efficiency—II." *Journal of Financial Economics* 6 (June–September 1978):297–330.

(2) Pettit, R. R. "Dividend Announcements, Security Performance and Capital Market Efficiency." *Journal of Finance* 27 (December 1972):993–1007.

Some studies of stock prices and the money supply:

(3)Auerbach, R. D. "Money and Stock Prices." *Monthly Review Federal Reserve Bank of Kansas City* (September–October 1976):3–11.

(4) Cooper, R. V. L. "Efficient Capital Markets and the Quantity Theory of Money." *Journal of Finance* 29 (June 1974):887–908.

(5) Hamburger, M. J., and Kochin, L. A. "Money and Stock Prices: The Channels of Influence." *Journal of Finance* 27 (May 1972):231–249.

(6) Homa, K. E., and Jaffee, D. M. "The Supply of Money and Common Stock Prices." *Journal of Finance* 26 (December 1971):1045–1066.

(7) Keran, M. W. "Expectations, Money and the Stock Market." *Review of the Federal Reserve Bank of Saint Louis* (June 1971):16–31.

(8) Palmer, M. "Money, Portfolio Adjustments and Stock Prices." *Financial Analysts Journal* 26 (July–August 1970):19–22.

(9) Pesando, J. E. "The Supply of Money and Common Stock Prices: Further Observations on the Econometric Evidence." *Journal of Finance* 29 (June 1974):909–922.

(10) Rogalski, R. J., and Vinso, J. D. "Stock Prices, Money Supply and the Direction of Causality." *Journal of Finance* 32 (September 1977):1017–1030.

(11) Rozeff, M. S. "Money and Stock Prices; Market Efficiency and the Lag in Effect of Monetary Policy." *Journal of Financial Economics* 1 (September 1974):245–302.

(12) Sprinkel, B. W. *Money and Stock Prices*. Homewood, Ill.: Richard D. Irwin, 1964.

(13) Tanner, J. E., and Trapani, J. M. "Can the Quantity Theory Be Used to Predict Stock Prices—Or Is the Stock Market Efficient?" *Southern Economic Journal* 44 (October 1977):261–290.

Some studies of the market reaction to stock splits (Walter's book is not concerned with testing efficiency but contains some interesting information on managers' reasons for splits):

(14) Ball, R., Brown, P., and Finn, F. "Share Capitalization Changes, Information, and the Australian Equity Market." *Australian Journal of Management* 2 (October 1977):105–117.

(15) Bar-Yosef, S., and Brown, L. D. "A Re-examination of Stock Splits Using Moving Betas." *Journal of Finance* 32 (September 1977):1069–1080.

(16) Charest, G. "Split Information, Stock Returns, and Market Efficiency." *Journal of Financial Economics* 6 (June–September 1978):256–296.

(17) Fama, E. F., Fisher, L., Jensen, M. C., and Roll, R. "The Adjustment of Stock Prices to New Information." *International Economic Review* 10 (February 1969):1–21.

(18) Foster, T. W., III, and Vickrey, D. "The Information Content of Stock Dividend Announcements." *Accounting Review* 53 (April 1978):360–370.

(19) Hausman, W. H., West, R. R., and Largay, J. A. "Stock Splits, Price Changes and Trading Profits: A Synthesis." *Journal of Business* 44 (January 1971):69–77.

(20) Nichols, W. D. "Security Price Reaction to Occasional Small Stock Dividends." *Financial Review* 16 (Winter 1981):54–62.

(21) Walter, J. E. *Dividend Policy and Enterprise Valuation.* Belmont, Calif.: Wadsworth Publishing Company, 1967.

Some studies of the effect on stock prices of large offers of stock:

(22) Carey, K. J. "Non Random Price Changes in Association with Trading in Large Blocks: Evidence of Market Efficiency in Behavior of Investors' Returns." *Journal of Business* 50 (1977):407–444.

(23) Dann, L. Y., Mayers, D., and Raab, R. J., Jr. "Trading Rules, Large Blocks and the Speed of Price Adjustment." *Journal of Financial Economics* 4 (January 1977):3–22.

(24) Grier, P. C., and Albin, P. S. "Non Random Price Changes in Association with Trading in Large Blocks." *Journal of Business* 46 (July 1973):425–433.

(25)Kraus, A., and Stoll, H. "Price Impacts of Block Trading on the New York Stock Exchange." *Journal of Finance* 27 (June 1972):569–588.

(26) Marsh, P. R. "Equity Rights Issues and the Efficiency of the UK Stock Market." *Journal of Finance* 34 (September 1979):839–862.

(27) Scholes, M. "The Market for Securities: Substitution versus Price Pressure and the Effects of Information on Share Prices." *Journal of Business* 45 (April 1972):179–211.

Some studies of the market reaction to other kinds of public information:

(28) Ball, R. J. "Changes in Accounting Technique and Stock Prices." *Empirical Research in Accounting: Selected Studies,* 1972. Supplement to *Journal of Accounting Research* 10 (1972):1–38.

(29) Ball, R. J., and Brown, P. "An Empirical Evaluation of Accounting Numbers." *Journal of Accounting Research* 6 (Autumn, 1968):159–178.

(30) Bradley, M. "Interfirm Tender Offers and the Market for Corporate Control." *Journal of Business* 53 (October 1980):345–376.

(31) Brown, S. "Earnings Changes, Stock Prices, and Market Efficiency." *Journal of Finance* 33 (March 1978):17–28.

(32) Dann, L. Y. "Common Stock Repurchases: An Analysis of Returns to Bondholders and Stockholders." *Journal of Finance* 9 (June 1981):113–138.

(33) Dodd, P. R. "Merger Proposals, Management Discretion and Stockholder Wealth." *Journal of Financial Economics* 8 (June 1980):105–138.

(34) Dodd, P. R., and Ruback, R. "Tender Offers and Stockholder Returns: An Empirical Analysis." *Journal of Financial Economics* 5 (1977):351–374.

(35) Finnerty, J. E. "Insiders and Market Efficiency." *Journal of Finance* 16 (September 1976): 1141–1148.

(36) Foster, G. "Stock Market Reaction to Estimates of Earnings per Share by Company Officials." *Journal of Accounting Research* 11 (1973):25–37.

(37) Grube, R. C., Joy, O. M., and Panton, D. "Market Responses to Federal Reserve Changes in the Initial Margin Requirement." *Journal of Finance* 34 (June 1979):659–674.

(38) Hillmer, S. C., and Yu, P. L. "The Market Speed of Adjustment to New Information." *Journal of Financial Economics* 7 (December 1979):321–346.

(39) Hopewell, M. H., and Schwartz, A. L., Jr. "Temporary Trading Suspensions in Individual NYSE Securities." *Journal of Finance* 33 (December 1978):1355–1373.

(40) Jaffe, J. F. "Special Information and Insider Trading." *Journal of Business* 47 (July 1974):410–429.

(41) Joy, M., Litzenberger, R., and McEnally, R. "The Adjustment of Stock Prices to Announcements of Unanticipated Changes in Quarterly Earnings." *Journal of Accounting Research* 15 (Autumn 1977):207–225.

(42) Kaplan, R. S., and Roll, R. "Investor Evaluation of Accounting Information: Some Empirical Evidence." *Journal of Business* 45 (April 1972):225–257.

(43) Largay, J. A., III, and West, R. R. "Margin Changes and Stock Price Behavior." *Journal of Political Economy* 81 (March–April 1973):328–339.

(44) Lorie, J. H., and Niederhoffer, V. 'Predictive and Statistical Properties of Insider Trading." *Journal of Law and Economics* 11 (April 1968):35–53.

(45) Mandelker, G. "Risk and Return: The Case of Merging Firms." *Journal of Financial Economics* 1 (December 1974):303–335.

(46) Masulis, R. W. "Stock Repurchase by Tender Offer: An Analysis of the Causes of Common Stock Price Changes." *Journal of Finance* 35 (1980):305–319.

(47) Patell, J. M. "Corporate Forecasts of Earnings per Share and Stock Price Behavior: Empirical Tests." *Journal of Accounting Research* 14 (Autumn 1976):246–276.

(48) Pinches, G. E., and Singleton, J. C. "The Adjustment of Stock Prices to Bond Rating Changes." *Journal of Finance* 33 (1978):29–44.

(49) Pratt, S. P., and De Vere, C. W. "Relationship between Insider Trading and Rates of Return for NYSE Common Stocks, 1960–66." In Lorie, J. H., and Brealey, R. A., eds., *Modern Developments in Investment Management*, 2nd ed., Hinsdale, Ill. Dryden Press, 1978.

(50) Reilly, F. K., and Drzycimski, E. F. "Tests of Stock Market Efficiency Following Major Events." *Journal of Business Research* 1 (Summer 1973):57–72.

(51) Vermaelen, T. "Common Stock Repurchases and Market Signalling: An Empirical Study." *Journal of Finance* 9 (June 1981):139–184.

(52) Waud, R. "Public Interpretation of Federal Reserve Discount Rate Changes: Evidence on the Announcement Effect." *Econometrica* 38 (March 1970):231–250.

(53) White, R. W., and Lusztig, P. A. "The Price Effects of Rights Offerings." *Journal of Financial and Quantitative Analysis* 15 (March 1980):25–40.

Fama's paper is a good general review of the literature on efficiency. Bagehot's paper is concerned with the role of the dealer:

(54) Bagehot, W. (pseud.) "The Only Game in Town." *Financial Analysts Journal* 27 (March–April 1971):12ff.

(55) Fama, E. F. "Efficient Capital Markets: A Review of Theory and Empirical Work." *Journal of Finance* 25 (May 1970):383–417.

3 Can Professional Investors Beat the Market?

In an efficient market, prices reflect all available information. We saw in the first chapter that there is considerable evidence that stock prices at least reflect the information contained in past prices. This weak form of efficiency implies that technical analysis is an unprofitable activity.

In the last chapter we saw that stock prices also impound other kinds of publicly available information. This "semi-strong" form of efficiency implies that it is impossible to earn consistently superior profits simply by a study of readily available information, such as the latest dividend or earnings or the president's annual statement.

In practice few professional analysts confine their attention to such basic items of information. The important remaining issue, therefore, is whether stock prices reflect not only publicly available information but any additional information that results from the tireless inquiries of professional security analysts. This would constitute a strong form of efficiency. It would indicate that no investor, however skilled, could earn superior profits other than by chance. Investment in such a market would be neither more nor less than a fair game.

Nobody believes literally in this strong form of the efficient market theory. The interesting question is how closely actual markets approximate such a visionary ideal.

Performance of Professionally Managed Portfolios

In a perfectly efficient market no portfolio manager could achieve consistently superior performance. Let us look therefore at some studies of whether professional managers can beat the market.

The classic study of investment performance examined the record of 115 mutual funds between 1955 and 1964.[1] The return on these funds depended not only on the ability of the manager to pick stocks but on the fund's volatility. Some of the mutual funds were invested in stable income stocks, which tended to maintain their value in bear markets but to lag in bull markets. Other mutual funds were invested in volatile growth stocks, which often had high returns in bull markets but performed badly in bear markets. Therefore, in order to measure the skill of each fund manager, it was necessary to abstract from the effect on the fund of general market movements. In order to do this, the return on the fund was compared with the return on an equally volatile package of the market index and risk-free debt.[2] Since the fund and the package had the same volatility, any consistent superiority in the fund's return should be due to the manager's skill in picking stocks.

In the case of the 115 mutual funds, the return before management expenses was on average 0.1 percent a year less than the return on an equally volatile package of the market index and risk-free debt. In other words, any gain from picking stocks was slightly more than offset by the transaction costs. Of course, some funds performed better than the average and others performed worse, but these differences were no greater than one would expect as a result of chance. There was no sign that *any* manager was able to achieve consistently superior performance.

Because mutual funds are so much in the public eye, they have been a popular object of performance studies. But other institutions do not seem to have performed any better. For example, the average abnormal returns before expenses on 1,200 portfolios managed by banks, insurance companies, investment counselors, and mutual funds (1968–1977) were −1.6, −1.1, −1.6, and −1.4 percent, respectively.[3] It is clear that mutual funds were not alone in failing to beat the market.

We should not claim too much precision for these studies of fund performance. We cannot be sure whether professional managers are likely to make very small percentage gains or (as it appears) very small percentage losses. We also cannot be sure whether there are any consistent differences between managers. Despite these cautions, it is clear from studies of fund performance that professional managers work in a very competitive environment and do not make large profits at the expense of the hapless amateur. It is equally clear that most of the differences between the performance of individual funds are the result of chance. These important conclusions are a warning against high ambition.

Stock Recommendations and Forecasts

While the performance record of investment managers is exactly what we should expect in an efficient market, it remains possible that analysts do have some power to forecast security prices. For example, it could be that managers ignore the advice of their analysts or act on it too late. Or perhaps their orders to buy or sell a stock forewarn other investors that the stock is mispriced. Or perhaps the purchases and sales are too small in value to add much to the performance of the total portfolio. Therefore, before we conclude that stock prices do indeed reflect all available information, we should look at the profitability of analysts' recommendations and forecasts.

One of the most extensive sources of analysts' recommendations is the *Wall Street Journal* column "Heard on the

Street." This column generally reports the opinions of several analysts about the same stock. For example, during 1970 and 1971 there were 785 occasions on which the column reported a unanimous recommendation to buy or sell stock. Figure 3.1 shows the relative performance of these stocks in the days surrounding publication.[4] Notice that when the stock is recommended for purchase, the price rises by about 1 percent on the publication day, whereas when it is recommended for sale, the price falls by about 2 percent. Although these price movements are scarcely dramatic, they do suggest that the analysts' forecasts have some modest value. As you can see from table 3.1, other studies of published investment advice point to a similar conclusion.

In addition to analyzing recommendations, it is also useful to examine the accuracy of analysts' forecasts. If the market is perfectly efficient and all information is impounded in the stock price, there should be no relationship between the forecast and actual returns. If it is not efficient and professional analysts do have superior information, there should be a positive correlation between the forecast and actual returns.

In June 1971 one financial institution analyzed the medium-term prospects for 250 stocks.[5] Each stock was rated on a scale of 1 to 5 in terms of its prospective performance relative to the rest of its industry. Thus the 15 stocks that the analysts placed in rank 1 were expected to perform worst; the 61 stocks that they placed in rank 2 were expected to offer somewhat below-average performance; and so on. Six months later the same stocks were again rated from 1 to 5 on the basis of their actual performance relative to their industry. Thus the 15 worst performers were placed in rank 1, the 61 next worst performers were assigned rank 2, and so on. If the analysts were perfect forecasters, there should have been an exact correspondence between the forecast rank and the actual rank; if they had no forecasting ability,

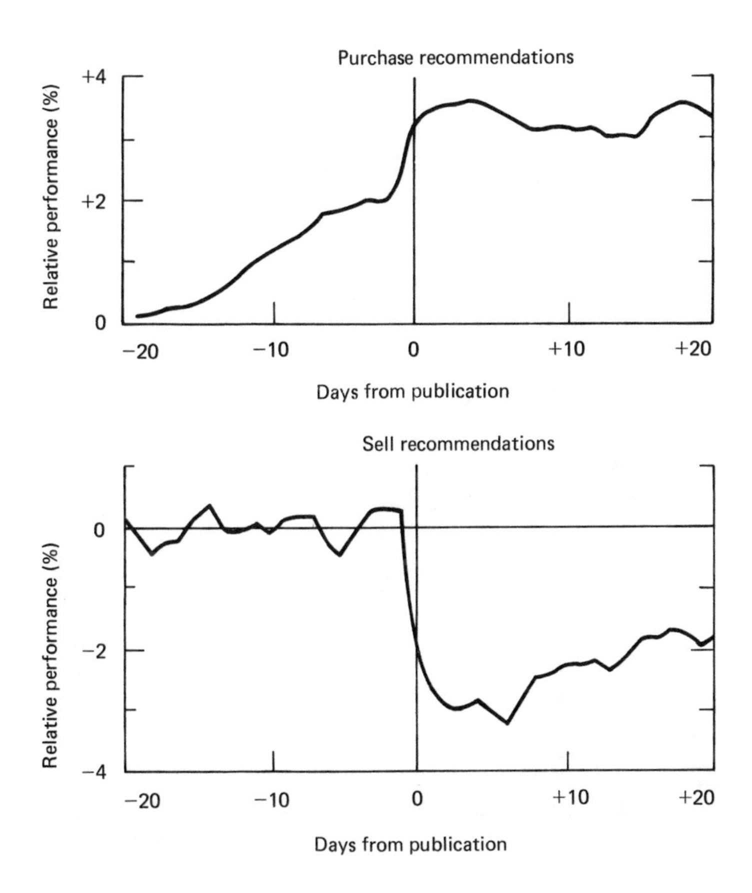

Figure 3.1
The relative performance of purchase and sell recommendations. From P. L. Davies and M. Canes, "Stock Prices and the Publication of Second-Hand Information," *Journal of Business* 51 (1978):43–56.

Table 3.1
Findings from studies of published investment advice

Author	Publication date	No. of advisory services	No. of recommendations	Percentage return on prepublication price		
				Publication day	After one week	Longer term
Cowles (14)	1933	45	7,500			− 1.4
Cowles (15)	1944	11	6,904			0.2
Ferber (18)	1958	4	345	0.5	1.1	
Ruff (21)	1963	1	31		4.0	
Colker (13)	1963	1	1,054			3.6
Stoffels (23)	1966	3	264	0.7	1.5	
Cheney (12)	1969	4				2.0
Diefenbach (17)	1972	24	1,209			2.7
Black (11)	1973	1	500			10.0
Logue and Tuttle (20)	1973	6	304			3.0
Groth et al. (19)	1979	1	6,014			2.6
Stanley et al. (22)	1981	1	4,461		0.7	
Bjerring et al. (10)	1982	1	80–92	1.5	1.2	

the correlation between the two sets of ranks should have been zero. In fact the correlation was 0.17, which suggests that the analysts had a small but significant degree of forecasting skill.

In a similar exercise sixteen investment firms provided ratings between 1972 and 1974 for about 150 stocks.[6] Over the subsequent four to seven months the correlation between the forecast and actual ranks averaged 0.16.

Finally, the same techniques have been used to assess the quality of investment advisory services.[7] Thus between 1973 and 1976 there was an average correlation of 0.07 between the Value Line stock rating and the actual outcome six months later, and there was an average correlation of 0.14 between Wells Fargo's stock rating and the actual outcome.

These direct studies of forecasting skill are somewhat more encouraging. They suggest that while the analysts' forecasts can explain only a small proportion of what subsequently happens, there is at least some relationship between the two. If this is so, the delicate problem is to translate such forecasts into superior portfolio performance. Unless the portfolio manager is aware of the amount of information in the analysts' forecasts, he is liable either to pass up profitable opportunities or to overreact and fritter away the gains in excessive transaction costs. Even if the manager does know exactly how much he should buy or sell on the strength of the forecasts, he still faces the difficulty of doing so without signaling his views to other investors.

Implications of the Efficient Market Theory

In the United States there are about 25 million common stock investors. Many of these may be inactive and others may be foolish, but there also undoubtedly exist many others who are both energetic and well informed. Given this competition, it would be surprising if important, available information went unnoticed for long.

It is this picture of a large number of investors competing to achieve similar ends that has prompted the suggestion that for the majority of the participants investment is a fair game. If this is indeed the case, you can easily match the performance of the average stockholder, but you need considerable skill to do better than this. Some investment institutions have, therefore, given up the attempt to obtain superior performance and have invested passively in a broad and representative sample of stocks. Although such a policy guarantees average performance at minimum cost, it would be stretching both theory and empirical evidence to insist that this is the only sensible portfolio strategy. If institutions must pay to obtain information, they will require some prospective reward before investing in security analysis. Moreover, although the studies of fund performance do not indicate that security analysis pays for itself in terms of portfolio performance, we have seen that there is slightly more encouraging evidence that professional security analysts have some forecasting ability.

If an institution is going to obtain superior performance, it will not be with the sole aid of public information, whether that information is the earnings record, management's most recent statment, or a brokerage firm's circular. Hence it is not sufficient to employ average analysts to do average things. One author has compared security analysis to a fairground game in which each player guesses the number of beans in a jar and wins only if his guess is better than the average of all other guesses.[8] This average guess represents the combined information of all the other players. So, if you wish to win such a game, you not only need to know more than any other single player, you need to know more than *all* other players.

Even though other players in the fairground game may individually make large errors, these errors will tend to cancel out as long as they are unrelated. Therefore, your only effective chance to win is if you notice that all the players are making the same mistake. When you play the security analysis game, you face a similar problem. As long as the stock price incorporates the information available to all other investors, you are unlikely to come up with a better assessment of the stock's worth simply by being more careful and more diligent. Your only chance of winning is to detect instances in which all analysts are relying on similar incorrect information sources.

If security analysis is to be effective, the organizational structure must encourage analysts to concentrate their attention on areas where they have a comparative advantage and focus on stocks where there is some chance of misvaluation. Neither condition is likely to be met if each analyst is compelled to comment at frequent intervals on a large number of securities.

These then are the primary conditions for superior investment performance. Yet it is important to bear in mind that in an efficient market the investment return is likely to depend far more on the risk that the fund assumes and more on its tax liability than on the accuracy of the analysts' forecasts. Thus the realization that markets are efficient has led institutions to focus more closely on the crucial aspects of risk and tax management.

Notes

1. See Jensen (3).

2. The rationale for measuring performance in this way is described in chapter 11.

3. See Bogle and Twardowski (1).

4. See Davies and Canes (16).

5. See Ambachtsheer (7).

6. See Ambachtsheer (8).

7. See Ambachtsheer and Farrell (9).

8. The bean jar analogy was suggested by Treynor.

References

Some studies of portfolio performance:

(1) Bogle, J. C., and Twardowski, J. M. "Institutional Investment Performance Compared: Banks, Investment Counselors, Insurance Companies, and Mutual Funds." *Financial Analysts Journal* 36 (January–February 1980):33–41.

(2) Friend, I., Blume, M. E., and Crockett, J. *Mutual Funds and Other Institutional Investors: A New Perspective.* New York: McGraw-Hill, 1970.

(3) Jensen, M. C. "The Performance of Mutual Funds in the Period 1945–1964." *Journal of Finance* 23 (May 1968):389–416.

(4) Kon, S. J., and Jen, F. C. "The Investment Performance of Mutual Funds: An Empirical Investigation of Timing, Selectivity and Market Efficiency." *Journal of Business* 52 (1979):263–289.

(5) U. S. Congress. *Institutional Investor Study Report of the Securities and Exchange Commission,* 92nd Congress, 1st session, 1971, H. Doc. No. 92–64.

(6) Williamson, J. P. "How Well are College Endowment Funds Managed?" *Journal of Portfolio Management* 6 (Summer 1979):19–22.

Some studies of the performance of analysts' forecasts:

(7) Ambachtsheer, K. P. "Portfolio Theory and the Security Analyst." *Financial Analysts Journal* 28 (November–December 1972):53–57.

(8) Ambachtsheer, K. P. "Profit potential in an 'Almost Efficient' Market." *Journal of Portfolio Management* 1 (Fall 1974):84–87.

(9) Ambachtsheer, K. P., and Farrell, J. L. "Can Active Management Add Value?" *Financial Analysts Journal* 35 (November–December 1979):39–48.

Some studies of the performance of analysts' recommendations:

(10) Bjerring, J. H., Lakonishok, J., and Vermaelen, T. "Stock Prices and Financial Analysts' Recommendations." *Journal of Finance,* forthcoming.

(11) Black, F. "Yes Virginia, There Is Hope: Tests of the Value Line Ranking System." *Financial Analysts Journal* 29 (September–October 1973):10–14.

(12) Cheney, H. L. "How Good Are Investment Advisory Services?" *Financial Executive* 37 (November 1969):30–35.

(13) Colker, S. S. "An Analysis of Security Recommendations by Brokerage Houses." *Quarterly Review of Economics and Business* 3 (Summer 1963):19–28.

(14) Cowles, A. "Can Stock Market Forecasters Forecast?" *Econometrica* 1 (July 1933):309–324.

(15) Cowles, A. "Stock Market Forecasting." *Econometrica* 12 (July–October 1944):206–214.

(16) Davies, P. L., and Canes, M. "Stock Prices and the Publication of Second-Hand Information." *Journal of Business* 51 (1978):43–56.

(17) Diefenbach, R. E. "How Good is Institutional Brokerage Research?" *Financial Analysts Journal* 28 (January–February 1972):54–60.

(18) Ferber, R. "Short Run Effects of Stock Market Services on Stock Prices." *Journal of Finance* 13 (March 1958):80–95.

(19) Groth, J. C., Lewellen, W. G., Schlarbaum, G. G., and Lease, R. C. "An Analysis of Brokerage House Recommendations." *Financial Analysts Journal* 35 (January–February 1979):32–40.

(20) Logue, D. E., and Tuttle, D. "Brokerage House Investment Advice." *Financial Review* (1973):38–54.

(21) Ruff, R. T. "The Effect of Selection and Recommendation of a Stock of the Month." *Financial Analysts Journal* 19 (March–April 1963): 41–43.

(22) Stanley, K. L., Lewellen, W. G., and Schlarbaum, G. G. "Further Evidence on the Value of Professional Investment Research." *Journal of Financial Research* 4 (Spring 1981):1–9.

(23) Stoffels, J. D. "Stock Recommendations by Investment Advisory Services: Immediate Effect on Market Pricing." *Financial Analysts Journal* 22 (March 1966):77–86.

II Valuation

4 Analyzing Common Stocks

The manager of any industrial firm will tell you how hard it is to earn more than a reasonable rate of return on the firm's investment. The message of chapters 1 to 3 is that it is equally hard to do so in the stock market. This is an important message because you are unlikely to be a successful investor unless you first face up to the difficulty of your task. With this in mind, we can now move on to consider the prerequisites for superior security analysis.

The Value of a Common Stock

Investors are a mercenary bunch, and they prize common stocks only for what they expect to get out of them. Suppose, for example, that you buy a share of IBM stock and hold it until the end of the year. Your total cash payoff would consist of the yearly dividend together with the price at which you subsequently sell the stock. If the stock is fairly valued, it must offer the same expected return as other stocks of similar risk. So the current price of IBM stock must equal the total expected payoff discounted by the return that investors expect to receive from similar stocks.

In order to value IBM stock, investors need to take three things into account: the return they require from their investment, the forecast dividend payment, and the forecast stock price at the end of the year. The tricky problem is to predict IBM's stock price at the end of the year. We know that at that point investors will need to go through the same valuation process as today. So the stock price at the end of the year will be equal to the discounted value of the dividend payment in year 2 and the expected stock price at the end of the second year. Likewise the stock price at the end of the second year will be equal to the discounted value of the expected dividend payment in year 3 and the expected stock price at the end of the third year. Therefore, instead of describing the value of IBM stock in terms of next year's dividend and stock price, we could say that it is equal to the discounted value of a continuing stream of expected dividend payments.[1]

How Far Ahead Do You Need to Forecast?

You sometimes hear it said that portfolio managers are nearsighted and focus on short-term price movements rather than on the long-term stream of dividends. But we have seen that next year's stock price depends on the prospective dividend payment in each subsequent year. Therefore, even if you expect to hold IBM stock for a short period only, you still cannot avoid thinking about the long-term outlook.

Obviously not all stocks offer the same dividend prospects. Some stocks are income stocks and are bought more for their high current yield than for their likely dividend growth. A large part of the value of an income stock, therefore, derives from the dividends that it is likely to pay in the next few years. By contrast, growth stocks pay relatively low dividends now but offer the prospect of much higher dividends in the future. Consequently, much of the value of a growth stock comes from these more distant dividends.

Figure 4.1 illustrates why the growth stock analyst needs to worry more about the distant future than the income stock analyst. For example, it shows that if a stock offers a current yield of 2 percent and a steady growth of 10 percent, then more than 80 percent of the stock's value derives from dividends beyond year 10. On the other hand, if a stock offers a current yield of 12 percent and no growth prospects, only 30 percent of its value comes from dividends beyond year 10.

Why Stock Prices Fluctuate

Security analysis would be a daunting task if you could value a stock only by projecting each dividend payment from now to kingdom come. Fortunately, it is sometimes possible to simplify the basic valuation formula. For example, suppose that dividends are expected to grow at a steady annual rate. In that case investors will expect the stock price to increase in line with the dividend, and the expected return will equal the dividend yield plus the expected rate of dividend growth:

$$\text{Expected return} = \frac{\text{forecast dividend}}{\text{price}} + \text{growth}.$$

This expression can be restructured to give the following formula for the price of a stock whose dividends are expected to grow at a steady rate:

$$\text{Price} = \frac{\text{forecast dividend}}{\text{expected return} - \text{growth}}.$$

This constant-growth formula makes it easy to see why quite small changes in the views of investors can lead to large variations in the stock price. For example, imagine that stock A is expected to pay a dividend next year of $2 and that the dividend is expected to grow indefinitely at an annual

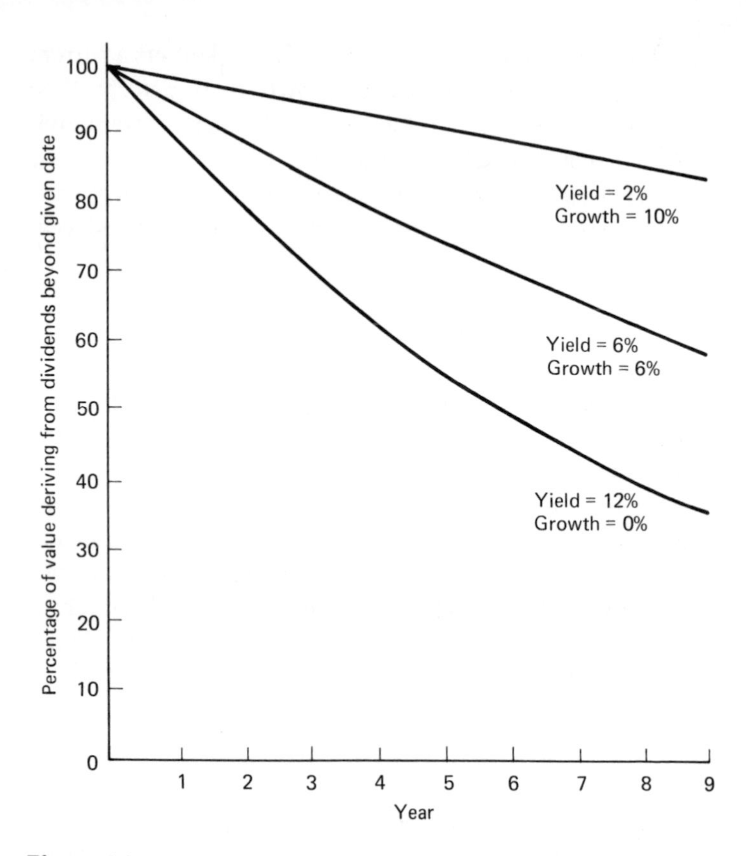

Figure 4.1
The proportion of a stock's value that derives from dividends beyond a given date depends on the stock's yield and its prospective dividend growth.

rate of 10 percent. If investors require a return on the stock of 12 percent, the current price will be $100.

$$\text{Price of A} = \frac{\text{dividend}}{\text{expected return} - \text{growth}}$$
$$= \frac{2}{.12 - .10} = \$100.$$

Now suppose that some news causes investors to reduce their forecast of dividend growth rate from 10 to 9 percent. Then the price of stock A will fall from $100 to $67:

$$\text{New price of A} = \frac{\text{dividend}}{\text{expected return} - \text{growth}}$$
$$= \frac{2}{.12 - .09} = \$67.$$

We can also understand why income stocks are less volatile than growth stocks. For instance, suppose that stock B is expected to pay a dividend next year of $10, but B's dividend is expected to grow by only 2 percent a year. If the expected return on the stock is 12 percent, the current price of stock B will also be $100:

$$\text{Price of B} = \frac{\text{dividend}}{\text{expected return} - \text{growth}}$$
$$= \frac{10}{.12 - .02} = \$100.$$

Now suppose that investors reduce their forecast of stock B's growth rate from 2 to 1 percent. Then the price of B will fall from $100 to $91:

$$\text{New price of B} = \frac{\text{dividend}}{\text{expected return} - \text{growth}}$$
$$= \frac{10}{.12 - .01} = \$91.$$

Thus a 1 percent reduction in the forecast dividend growth leads to a 33 percent fall in the price of growth stock A but only a 9 percent fall in that of income stock B.

An improvement in economic prospects or a fall in the return that investors require will lead to a widespread rise in stock prices. But this rise is likely to be more marked in the case of growth stocks than income stocks. Do not be misled into believing that investors are simply slow to appreciate the superior prospects of the growth companies.[2]

Inflation and Stock Prices

Since common stocks represent a claim against real assets, they have traditionally been regarded as an ideal hedge against inflation. Unfortunately, the chilling truth is that equities have performed rather less well when inflation is low than when it is high.[3]

Nobody knows for sure why this is the case, but there are several possible explanations. One is that inflation has been accompanied by a decline in the real level of company cash flows, perhaps because inflation is often associated with low levels of industrial activity or because the depreciation deduction does not rise with inflation. A second possibility is that during periods of inflation investors require a higher real interest rate and, therefore, a higher real return on their equities. A third view is that the fall in equity prices is not caused by either a fall in the real level of the company's dividend stream or a rise in the required real return. Instead, it is argued, the poor performance of equities in periods of high inflation results from an error in the way that investors evaluate them.[4]

To see how this valuation error could come about, suppose that in a noninflationary world a company is expected to pay each year a dividend of $1 a share. Since this dividend is not expected to grow, the stock price is simply equal to the forecast dividend divided by the required rate of return. For example, if investors require a return of 5 percent a year, the stock price would be

$$\frac{1.00}{.05} = \$20$$

Now suppose that investors foresee an annual inflation rate of 10 percent. If the company's real profits are unaffected, the forecast dividend will rise in line with inflation. In addition, if investors continue to demand the same real rate of return from their investment, the required nominal return must also rise with the prospective inflation rate. Therefore, the value of the stock will be equal to the stream of inflated dividends discounted by the inflated required return:

$$\frac{1.00 \times 1.10}{1.05 \times 1.10} + \frac{1.00 \times 1.10^2}{1.05^2 \times 1.10^2} + \cdots = \frac{1.00}{.05} = \$20.$$

In other words, the current stock price will be unchanged as long as investors remember to discount the real dividend payment of $1 by the 5 percent required real return. But perhaps they do not remember. Perhaps they look only at the high nominal rates of interest and forget that the dividend stream is also likely to rise with inflation. In that case, the prospect of inflation would cause stock prices to fall.

The notion that investors discount the real dividend stream by a nominal discount rate is a very controversial one and certainly does not square well with the idea that markets are efficient. But at least it is a useful reminder that we should be careful not to confuse high nominal rates of interest with high real rates.

Do Stock Prices Fluctuate Too Much?

Although quite small changes in a stock's prospects can cause substantial variations in the price, some investors believe that in practice price fluctuations are too large to be justified in this way.

Suppose, for example, that a hundred or so years ago an investor had unwittingly made a correct forecast of future dividends and had discounted them back to arrive at an estimate of equity values. Suppose also that he had repeated this exercise in each subsequent year using the same real discount rate. The dotted line in figure 4.2 shows how much his estimates of value would have fluctuated in real terms around their long-run trend. For comparison the solid line in figure 4.2 shows how market prices have in fact fluctuated in real terms around their trend. The volatility of actual market prices appears to have been far greater than can be explained by fluctuations in dividends.[5]

Each year's dividend announcements not only tell you what dividends are that year, they also provide some clues about likely future payments. It is this new information that leads to unexpected changes in price. But since 1870 the unexpected variations in stock market prices have been about five times greater than could result simply from the news that is contained in the annual dividend payments. Thus, once again it appears that market movements have been considerably larger than the changing outlook for future dividends could justify.

These calculations do not necessarily imply that market fluctuations are unjustifiably large. It could be that the real rate of return that investors use to discount prospective dividends also changes rapidly over time. But it does seem that there is more to predicting stock prices than just thinking about the dividend outlook.

One Approach to Security Analysis

The principal object of security analysis is to uncover stocks that offer an unusually high expected return for their level of risk.

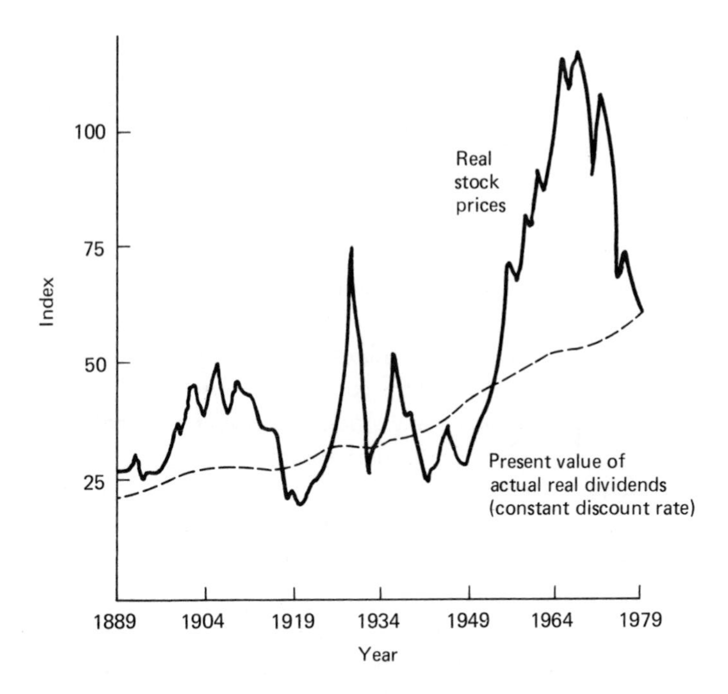

Figure 4.2
The actual fluctuations in market prices (solid line) have been much larger than the fluctuations in the discounted value of future dividends (dotted line). From S. J. Grossman and R. J. Shiller, "The Determinants of the Variability of Stock Market Prices," *American Economic Review* 71 (May 1981):222–227.

Most security analysts rely largely on hunches and rules of thumb to trap these elusive creatures, but some analysts attempt to apply the basic stock valuation formula described earlier. In order to do this, you first need to forecast the stock's future dividend payments. Of course, you cannot hope to predict separately the dividend payment for every future year, but it may be possible to predict the dividend for each of the next several years and then estimate the average rate of growth thereafter. Once you have made an estimate of future dividends, you can calculate the likely return from the stock. If the forecasted return is higher than that of other equally risky stocks, then you have some evidence that the stock is undervalued.[6]

When you do find a stock that seems to offer a particularly high or low return, then it is probable that your forecast of future dividends is different from the market's forecast. There are two reasons that this could be so. First, if you have made a detailed analysis of the company, you may well have learned something about its prospects that the market does not know. Unfortunately, however diligent you have been, it is also possible that the market knows something that you do not know. The danger is that the second source of disagreement may be much more important than the first. In this case, you may find that much of the time you will buy and sell stocks on the basis of your errors rather than the market's errors.

This danger also besets analysts who use cruder rules of thumb to value securities. For example, most institutions produce earnings forecasts for the companies that they follow. If your forecast is higher than the Street forecast, it is tempting to believe that this must reflect some information that you possess. It is easy to forget that it may also reflect information that only others possess. If you buy and sell stocks on the basis of a comparison between your earnings forecast and the consensus forecast, you are likely to find that much of the time you are trading on the basis of your forecast errors.

A Second Approach to Security Analysis

Suppose you have information that leads you to believe that the market is underestimating sales of Ford's new compact car. There are two ways in which you could use that information. The first would be to forecast Ford's future stream of dividends and then calculate the expected return from the common stock. Your set of dividend forecasts would incorporate your information about sales of the new compact, but it would also take into account your views about sales of other models, manufacturing costs, future capital expenditures, and so on. Despite your information about the new compact, it is quite possible that you may conclude that Ford stock offers a lower return than securities of similar risk.

An alternative approach would be to value only the information that you believe the market does not possess. In other words, rather than trying to develop a comprehensive view of Ford's prospects, you could simply ask yourself how much those extra sales would add to the value of the stock.

In this case you do not need to worry whether the market knows things that you do not. On the other hand, you do have to make sure that your knowledge is not already public, for if everybody shares your view that Ford's compact is a winner, the stock will no longer be cheap.

Implications for the Organization

These two contrasting approaches to security analysis have very different implications for the way that the research and dealing departments of an investment firm are organized.[7] The first approach takes the analyst's forecasts of future dividends and produces an estimate of each stock's expected return or value. It makes sense when an analyst is well placed to judge what others know and has some skill in processing that information. But in order to obtain a consistent set of dividend forecasts, it is also necessary to have a well-structured research department in which analysts are not free to follow each passing whim.

If you follow this approach to security analysis, you will wish to buy a stock only so long as its price is less than the estimated value. Therefore, you should set a limit on the price that you are prepared to pay and you should continue to add to your holding if the stock price falls further below its estimated value.

Investors who follow the second approach to security analysis are not concerned with valuing the information that is already known to the market. Their task is to identify and value only those items of information that the market does not yet possess. In this case the research department does not need to be highly structured and it can happily accommodate the nonconformist and the eccentric.

If you follow this second approach, you will never have your own view of the stock's value. You will know only that the stock price is likely to rise when other investors come to share your knowledge. Therefore, there is little point in setting buying limits or in buying more stock as the price falls. Instead, you should be prepared to deal at the market price and you should make sure that you cease to buy as soon as the knowledge has become public.

Notes

1. This discounted cash flow formula was first suggested in 1938 by J. B. Williams (4). Some of its important implications were discussed in 1961 by Miller and Modigliani (2).

2. This was pointed out by Treynor (3).

3. The references include a number of tests of the relationship between stock prices and inflation and some discussion of the findings.

4. See Modigliani and Cohn (14).

5. See the papers by Shiller (24, 25) and Grossman and Shiller (22).

6. Instead of comparing your forecasts of return, you could equally well discount the expected dividend payments to provide an estimate of each stock's value. Whether you work in terms of estimated returns or estimated values is largely a matter of taste. For an example of the application of these discounted cash flow models, see Fouse (1).

7. These two approaches to security analysis and their implications for dealing were suggested by Treynor (26).

References

Some discussions and applications of the "discounted dividends" formula:

(1) Fouse, W. L. "Risk and Liquidity: The Keys to Stock Price Behavior." *Financial Analysts Journal* 32 (May–June 1976):35–45.

(2) Miller, M. H., and Modigliani, F. "Dividend Policy, Growth and the Valuation of Shares." *Journal of Business* 34 (October 1961):411–433.

(3) Treynor, J. L. "Editor's Comment." *Financial Analysts Journal* 29 (November–December 1973):6.

(4) Williams, J. B. *The Theory of Investment Value*. Cambridge Mass.: Harvard University Press, 1938.

Some studies of the effect of inflation on stock prices:

(5) Alchian, A. A., and Kessel, R. "Redistribution of Wealth through Inflation." *Science* (September 1959):535–539.

(6) Arak, M. "Inflation and Stock Values: Is Our Tax Structure the Villain?" *Quarterly Review Federal Reserve Bank of New York* 5 (Winter 1980–1981):3–13.

(7) Bodie, Z. "Common Stocks as a Hedge against Inflation." *Journal of Finance* 31 (May 1976):459–470.

(8) Brealey, R. A. "Inflation and the Real Value of Government Assets." *Financial Analysts Journal* 35 (January–February 1979):18–21.

(9) Cagan, P. *Common Stock Values and Inflation—The Historical Record of Many Countries.* National Bureau of Economic Research, Report No. 13, March 1974.

(10) Fama, E. F., and Schwert, G. W. "Asset Returns and Inflation." *Journal of Financial Economics* 5 (1977):115–146.

(11) Jaffee, J., and Mandelker, G. " 'The Fisher Effect' for Risky Assets: An Empirical Investigation." *Journal of Finance* 31 (May 1976):447–470.

(12) Hong H. "Inflation and the Market Value of the Firm: Theory and Empirical Tests." *Journal of Finance* 32 (September 1977):1031–1048.

(13) Lintner, J. "Inflation and Security Returns." *Journal of Finance* 30 (May 1975):259–280.

(14) Modigliani, F., and Cohn, R. A. "Inflation, Rational Valuation and the Market." *Financial Analysts Journal* 35 (March–April 1979):24–44.

(15) Moore, B. "Equity Values and Inflation: The Importance of Dividends." *Lloyds Bank Review* (July 1980):1–15.

(16) Moosa, S. A. "Inflation and Common Stock Prices.' *Journal of Financial Research* 3 (Fall 1980):115–128.

(17) Nelson, C. R. "Inflation and Rates of Return on Common Stocks." *Journal of Finance* 31 (May 1976):471–483.

(18) Oudet, B. A. "The Variation of the Return on Stocks in Periods of Inflation." *Journal of Financial and Quantitative Analysis* 8 (March 1973):247–258.

(19) Reilly, F. K., Johnson, G. L., and Smith, R. E. "Inflation, Inflation Hedges and Common Stocks." *Financial Analysts Journal* 26 (January–February 1970):104–110.

(20) Schwert, G. W. "The Adjustment of Stock Prices to Information about Inflation." *Journal of Finance* 36 (March 1981):15–29.

(21) Van Horne, J. C., and Glassmire, W. F., Jr. "The Impact of Changes in Inflation on the Value of Common Stocks." *Journal of Finance* 27 (September 1972):1081–1092.

Some studies that discuss whether stock prices fluctuate too much:

(22) Grossman, S. J., and Shiller, R. J. "The Determinants of the Variability of Stock Market Prices." *American Economic Review* 71 (May 1981):222–227.

(23) LeRoy, S. F., and Porter, R. D. "The Present-Value Relation: Tests Based on Implied Variance Bounds." *Econometrica* 49 (1981):555–574.

(24) Shiller, R. J. "Do Stock Prices Move Too Much to Be Justified by Subsequent Changes in Dividends?" *American Economic Review* 71 (June 1981):421–436.

(25) Shiller, R. J. "The Use of Volatility Measures in Assessing Market Efficiency." *Journal of Finance* 36 (May 1981):291–303.

This paper discusses alternative trading strategies:

(26) Treynor J. L. "What Does It Take to Win the Trading Game." *Financial Analysts Journal* 37 (January–February 1981):55–60.

5 The Behavior of Earnings

An unexpected change in company earnings provides important information about the likely future stream of dividends, so it is not surprising that there is a strong association between unexpected changes in earnings and changes in the stock price. For example, table 5.1 lists the twenty NYSE stocks showing the greatest price appreciation in 1970. It also lists the earnings changes that were forecast by leading financial institutions and the changes that subsequently occurred. Table 5.2 provides similar information for the twenty NYSE stocks showing the greatest price falls in 1970. The recipe for investment success is clear: buy the stock if investors are substantially underestimating future earnings and sell it if investors are substantially overestimating earnings. Unfortunately earnings changes are not so easy to predict.

What's in an Earnings Record?

Companies with superior rates of earnings growth often owe their success to some monopoly power. They may possess unique management skills or technological know-how or a sales force that allows them to grow at the expense of their rivals. In other cases their advantage may derive from the high costs and long start-up times that are faced by would-be new entrants to the industry. Even in a dynamic and

Table 5.1
Twenty best percentage price changes in 1970

	Earnings per share ($)			Stock price
NYSE stocks	Actual 1969	Est. 1970	Actual 1970	Actual % change
1. Overnight Transportation	1.47	1.47	2.58	+125.0
2. Coca-Cola Bottling, N.Y.	1.08	1.18	1.30	84.2
3. Bates Manufacturing	0.02		1.28	72.6
4. General Cigar	2.24	2.30	3.01	70.5
5. Texas East Transmission	2.40	2.50	2.70	70.5
6. Credithrift Financial	1.07		1.15	63.6
7. Green Shoe Mfg.	1.93	2.20	2.60	63.6
8. Pittston Co.	1.11	1.67	2.20	63.6
9. Campbell Red Lake Mining	0.73	0.65	0.48	62.3
10. Blue Bell	3.13	3.70	3.81	60.0
11. Collins & Aikman	2.47	2.50	2.61	59.2
12. Gamble-Skogmo	2.66	2.60	3.08	57.1
13. Amerada Hess	2.41	2.55	3.22	56.0
14. Giant Portland Cement	0.71		1.07	55.1
15. AMF, Inc.	1.85	2.00	2.05	54.7
16. Rubbermaid, Inc.	1.28	1.40	1.44	54.2
17. Cone Mills Corp.	0.97	1.20	1.51	53.6
18. Graniteville Co.	1.29	1.30	2.07	52.5
19. Keebler	2.01	2.10	2.95	51.8
20. Interco	3.13	2.80	3.31	51.6

Source: After V. Niederhoffer and P. J. Regan, "Earnings Changes, Analysts' Forecasts, and Stock Prices," *Financial Analysts Journal* 28 (May–June 1972):65–71.

Table 5.2
Twenty worst percentage price changes in 1970

	Earnings per share			Stock price
NYSE stocks	Actual 1969	Est. 1970	Actual 1970	Actual % change
1. Penn Central	0.18	2.00	d13.67	−77.9
2. University Computing	2.58		d 1.28	−77.7
3. Electronic Mem. & Mag.	0.93	1.05	d 2.12	−76.9
4. Fairchild Camera	0.23	1.00	d 4.40	−74.7
5. Scientific Resources	d0.78		d 1.40	−72.7
6. Transcontinental Invest.	0.60	1.30	d 0.62	−72.5
7. FAS International	0.92	1.10	0.39	−71.1
8. Republic Corp	1.48	2.75	0.23	−68.2
9. Sonesta	0.27		d 1.17	−68.0
10. Automation Industries	0.81	1.20	0.22	−62.9
11. GAC Corp	3.22	4.00	1.62	−62.9
12. Sprague Electric	0.43	0.75	d 1.78	−61.8
13. Memorex	1.87	2.50	0.83	−61.0
14. Ward Foods	1.84		0.40	−60.6
15. Whittaker Corp	1.51	1.25	0.28	−59.2
16. Ling-Temco-Vought	d0.05		d12.73	−59.1
17. Dictaphone	1.09	1.15	d 0.74	−58.4
18. MEI Corp	d0.19		d 0.05	−58.3
19. Smith International	1.63	1.75	0.98	−58.2
20. Standard Pressed Steel	0.73	0.70	d 1.10	−58.1

Source: V. Niederhoffer and P. J. Regan, "Earnings Changes, Analysts' Forecasts, and Stock Prices," *Financial Analysts Journal* 28 (May–June 1972):65–71.

competitive economy such advantages are unlikely to vanish overnight. Therefore, we might expect that companies with good earnings growth would experience higher subsequent rates of growth than those with bad records.

One simple test of this possibility considered 610 companies with a continuous record of earnings over fourteen years. Companies were first grouped according to the number of years in which they were among the top 305 firms in terms of earnings growth. The result is shown in the second column of table 5.3. Notice, for example, that no company was in the top half of the class in each of the fourteen years, and only one company was in the top half for thirteen out of fourteen years. The third column of table 5.3 shows the number of companies that could be expected to fall into each group if the god of economics had distributed his largesse with a pepper pot. The actual number of companies in each group is very similar to the chance distribution.

We can also determine whether for each company the good or bad years tended to bunch together. For this purpose the 610 companies were strung together in random order to form a chain of 8,540 good or bad earnings changes. The second column of table 5.4 shows the number of instances of a run of only one good year, two successive good years, and so on. The number of runs of bad years are shown in the third column. These figures may be compared with the final column, which shows the corresponding distribution that would have been produced by the wanton god with the pepper pot. Instead of a company's good or bad years bunching together, there is a slight reverse tendency. With the possible exception of companies that experienced a very long run of success, a good year or a succession of good years was more frequently followed by a bad year and vice versa.

This simple test merely examined whether a company was in the top or bottom half of the class but otherwise took no

Table 5.3
Number of companies experiencing a given number of years' growth in excess of midvalue

Number of good years	Actual number of companies	Expected number of companies
0	0	0
1	0	1
2	1	3
3	6	14
4	34	37
5	84	75
6	114	112
7	139	128
8	115	112
9	68	75
10	30	37
11	16	14
12	2	3
13	1	1
14	0	0

Source: R. A. Brealey, "The Statistical Properties of Successive Changes in Earnings," paper presented to the Seminar on the Analysis of Security Prices, University of Chicago, May 1967.

account of the size of the earnings change. An alternative approach is to draw a scatter diagram such as figure 5.1. The horizontal axis represents the percentage growth in earnings per share in one year; the vertical axis marks the growth in the next year. Each cross depicts the experience of a different company. If some companies are consistently more successful than others, the crosses should tend to form an upward-sloping line as in figure 5.1. The correlation coefficient is a measure of this tendency. A positive correlation would indicate that the crosses tend to cluster along an upward-sloping line. A correlation of zero would suggest that they are scattered haphazardly.

Table 5.5 shows the correlation coefficients between the earnings changes of approximately 700 companies for thirteen pairs of adjacent years. There is no sign here that growth tends to be repeated; if anything, there is a slight tendency for the best performing companies one year to be among the laggards the next year. The earnings changes of the 700 companies in one year were also compared with the changes two years later. Just as in the case of the adjacent years, the correlations are for the most part slightly negative.

This test, like the previous one, defined good and bad relative to the performance of a group of companies. A different picture might emerge if a company's growth was measured relative to the company's own performance in other periods. Thus for each company we can draw a scatter diagram like figure 5.2. The horizontal axis represents that company's growth in one year; the vertical axis represents the change over the succeeding year. Each cross depicts the experience in a different pair of years. If earnings growth does indeed persist, the crosses would tend to cluster along an upward-sloping line and the correlation between successive changes would be positive. To see whether this is the case, a study was made of 217 companies with unbroken earnings records from 1948 to 1966. On average the correlation between successive earnings changes was −.13.

Table 5.4
Runs of successive years with growth greater or less than midvalue

Length of run (years)	Actual number of runs of good years	Actual number of runs of bad years	Expected number of runs of good or bad years
1	1,152	1,102	1,068
2	562	590	534
3	266	300	267
4	114	120	133
5	55	63	67
6	24	20	33
7	23	12	17
8	5	6	8
9	3	3	4
10	6	0	2
11	2	0	1
12	1	0	1
13	0	0	0
14	0	1	0

Source: R. A. Brealey, "The Statistical Properties of Successive Changes in Earnings," paper presented to the Seminar on the Analysis of Security Prices, University of Chicago, May 1967.

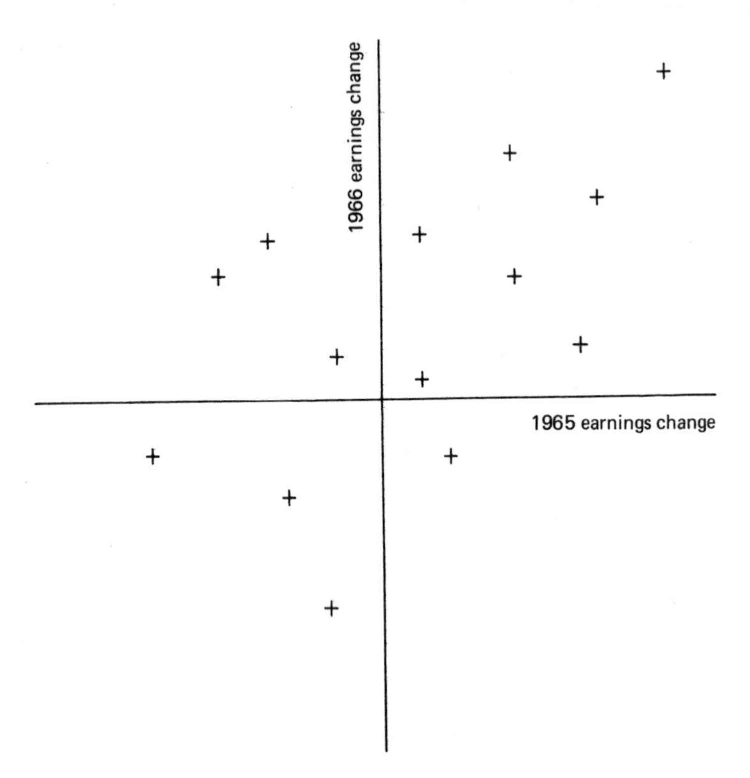

Figure 5.1
Each cross in this scatter diagram shows the earnings changes of a different company in the years 1965 and 1966.

Table 5.5
Correlation coefficients between earnings changes of all companies for adjacent years

	1952 and 1951	1953 and 1952	1954 and 1953	1955 and 1954	1956 and 1955	1957 and 1956	1958 and 1957
Coefficient	−0.15	−0.04	−0.08	−0.20	0.03	−0.01	0.17

	1959 and 1958	1960 and 1959	1961 and 1960	1962 and 1961	1963 and 1962	1964 and 1963	Average
Coefficient	−0.26	−0.14	−0.12	0	−0.02	0.03	−0.06

Source: R. A. Brealey, "The Statistical Properties of Successive Changes in Earnings," paper presented to the Seminar on the Analysis of Security Prices, University of Chicago, May 1967.

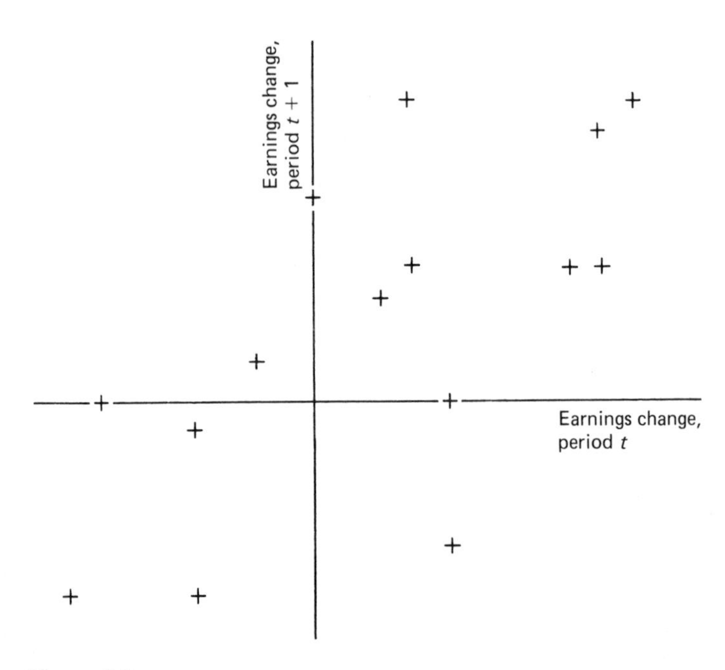

Figure 5.2
Each cross in this scatter diagram shows the earnings changes of one hypothetical company in successive years.

When each year's change was compared with the change two years later, the average correlation was −.09.

Contrary to the original suggestion, these and similar tests all show a slight tendency for a good short-term earnings gain to be reversed. It is difficult to believe that some companies do not have a persistent competitive advantage. It seems therefore as if these enduring features are swamped by the impact of nonrecurring events. For example, if progress is interrupted one year by destruction of the plant by fire, the record would include one year of sharp earnings fall succeeded by a correspondingly sharp recovery. Thus windfall events of this kind will have the opposite effect of monopolistic advantages and will lead to frequent reversals in the rate of earnings growth.

Windfall events are likely to be of less importance over the longer term. Despite this, comparison of earnings growth trends in successive five-year periods also revealed little conformity. Presumably, over these longer periods, monopolies crumble and the forces making for persistence in earnings progress diminish.

Although *changes* in both earnings and stock prices are approximately random, it is important to stress that neither result is conditional on the other. In particular, it would be quite possible for earnings to describe an ordered progression and for stock prices to move randomly. After all, the prime condition for the random character of stock price movement is simply that no limited group of investors should have a monopoly of knowledge.

Although analysts are in part able to forecast earnings changes, their task is not made easier by the fact that the past earnings record is little or no guide to the future. The temptation to extrapolate earnings is insidious, particularly when other information is scanty and time is pressing. A study of the five-year earnings forecasts made by five institutions suggested that, to a considerable extent, these forecasts consisted of extrapolations of past rates of growth. A similar tendency seems to be evident in short-term forecasts. It is at best a valueless procedure and may distract attention from more relevant information.[1]

Common Influences in Earnings Changes

When the wind of recession blows, there are few companies that do not lean with it. In consequence, aggregate corporate profits tend to rise and fall in line with economic activity.

Not all companies, however, are equally dependent for their well-being on a good business climate. At one end of the spectrum, the profits of such companies as auto or steel producers are determined to a considerable extent by the general level of prosperity. In contrast, demand for such essential commodities as cigarettes, beer, and cosmetics is almost wholly unresponsive to recession.

Some attempt has been made to quantify these differences for a sample of companies divided into twenty industry groups. The second column of table 5.6 shows for each industry group the proportion of the variation in company earnings changes that could be explained in terms of a common influence. On average 21 percent of the movement in company earnings could be attributed to variations in the fortunes of the corporate sector as a whole, but there were considerable differences between industries. At one extreme, the earnings of cosmetic firms were almost unaffected by economy-wide changes in profits. At the other extreme, almost half of the movement in the earnings of automobile companies could be explained in terms of the common influence. Clearly, the analyst's success in forecasting an automobile company's profits must depend in large measure on his ability to predict the course of aggregate corporate profits.

The profits of companies in the same industry are likely to move in closer unison than those of companies in different industries. The more homogeneous the product and manufacturing process, the more important should be this industry influence. Thus we might expect a much closer association between the earnings changes of a group of oil companies than between those of a group of drug manufacturers.

The third column of table 5.6 shows the additional proportion of earnings fluctuations that could be explained in terms of the company's industry membership. For example, it indicates that a large part of the task of forecasting oil or rubber company earnings lies in an understanding of the outlook for the industry as a whole. This type of approach

Table 5.6
Proportion of earnings movement attributable to common or industry influences

Industry	Common influence (%)	Industry influence (%)
Aircraft	11	5
Autos	48	11
Beer	11	7
Cement	6	32
Chemicals	41	8
Cosmetics	5	6
Department stores	30	37
Drugs	14	7
Electricals	24	8
Food	10	10
Machinery	19	16
Nonferrous metals	26	25
Office machinery	14	6
Oil	13	49
Paper	27	28
Rubber	26	48
Steel	32	21
Supermarkets	6	33
Textiles and clothing	25	29
Tobacco	8	19
All companies	21	21

Source: R. A. Brealey, "Some Implications of the Comovement of American Company Earnings," *Applied Economics* 3 (1971):183–196.

is impossible with cosmetics or aircraft firms; the prospects for these companies can be analyzed only on an individual basis.[2] Thus, the type of skills that the analyst needs and the way that research responsibilities are allocated depends on the factors that influence each company's profits.

Notes

1. The random character of earnings changes was first observed by Little for U.K. companies. See, for example, Little and Rayner (9). The tests described earlier are taken from Brealey (6).

2. These tests were taken from Brealey (5). See Foster (12) for further evidence on the comovement of earnings and for an excellent general review of the literature on the behavior of earnings.

References

The following paper illustrates the effect on stock prices of unexpected earnings announcements. Some other analyses are listed in the references for chapter 2:

(1) Niederhoffer, V., and Regan, P. J. "Earnings Changes, Analysts' Forecasts, and Stock Prices." *Financial Analysts Journal* 28 (May–June 1972):65–71.

Some studies of the behavior of annual earnings:

(2) Albrecht, W. S., Lookabill, L. L., and McKeown, J. C. "The Time-Series Properties of Annual Earnings." *Journal of Accounting Research* 15 (Autumn 1977):226–244.

(3)Ball, R. J., and Watts, R. "Some Time Series Properties of Accounting Income." *Journal of Finance* 27 (June 1972):663–682.

(4) Beaver, W. H. "The Time Series Behavior of Earnings." *Empirical Research in Accounting: Selected Studies.* Supplement to *Journal of Accounting Research* 8 (1970):62–99.

(5)Brealey, R. A. "Some Implications of the Comovement of American Company Earnings."*Applied Economics* 3 (1971):183–196.

(6) Brealey, R. A. "The Statistical Properties of Successive Changes in Earnings." Paper presented to the Seminar on the Analysis of Security Prices. University of Chicago, May 1967.

(7) Dopuch, N., and Watts, R. L. "Using Time-Series Models to Assess the Significance of Accounting Changes." *Journal of Accounting Research* 10 (Spring 1972):180–194.

(8) Lintner, J., and Glauber, R. "Higgledy, Piggledy Growth in America." In J. H. Lorie and R. A. Brealey, eds., *Modern Developments in Investment Management*, 2nd ed. Hinsdale, Ill.: The Dryden Press, 1978.

(9) Little, I. M. D., and Rayner, A. C. *Higgledy Piggledy Growth Again*. Oxford: Basil Blackwell, 1966.

(10) Lookabill, L. L. "Some Additional Evidence on the Time Series Properties of Accounting Signals." *Accounting Review* 51 (October 1976):724–738.

(11) Watts, R. L., and Leftwich, R. W. "The Time Series of Annual Accounting Earnings." *Journal of Accounting Research* 15 (Autumn 1977):253–271.

Foster's book provides an excellent review of the literature on the behavior and comovement of earnings:

(12) Foster, G. *Financial Statement Analysis*. Englewood Cliffs, N.J.: Prentice-Hall, 1978.

III Choosing a Common Stock Portfolio

6 Portfolio Selection

Many portfolio managers view their function as that of a superior security analyst graciously accepting or rejecting the recommendations of subordinate analysts. But if you are to be a successful portfolio manager, you not only need good security analysts, you also need to decide how much to bet on their ideas. If the bets are too small, you will be wasting the benefits of the security analysis; if they are too large, you risk heavy losses if matters do not work out as you expect. Thus the main role of the portfolio manager is to choose a portfolio that offers the best trade-off between expected return and risk. Modern portfolio theory tells the manager how to make this trade-off.

Choosing Efficient Portfolios

The solid line in figure 6.1 shows what has happened to the price of Zenith common stock between 1975 and 1981. The wide price fluctuations made Zenith a very risky stock. If you were fortunate and bought at the bottom in 1980, you would have made a large profit; if you were unfortunate and bought at the peak in 1976, you would have suffered a large loss.

Statisticians often measure variability by the standard deviation. The variability, or standard deviation, of the returns

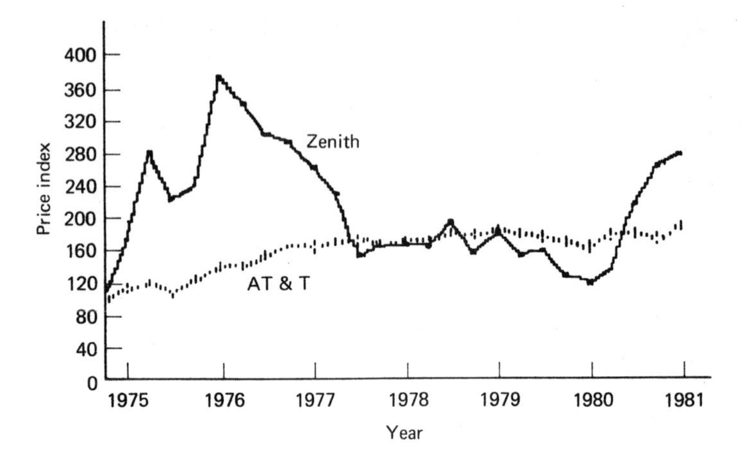

Figure 6.1
Prices of Zenith and AT&T stocks.

on Zenith stock was 55 percent a year. This implies that approximately one year in three the return on Zenith stock was at least 55 percent higher than expected or 55 percent lower.

The dotted line in figure 6.1 shows the price movement of AT&T stock. While AT&T was by no means a safe investment, its returns were substantially less variable than Zenith's. In fact its variability, or standard deviation, was 12 percent a year. Roughly one year in three the return on AT&T stock would have been at least 12 percent better than investors expected or 12 percent worse.

Figure 6.1 also shows that the fortunes of Zenith and AT&T were not perfectly related. There were many occasions when the price of one stock rose while that of the other fell. Because the stocks did not move in exact lockstep, you could have reduced the variability of your investment by putting money in each stock. For example, if you had divided your investment evenly between the two stocks, the variability of the returns on your portfolio would have been 30 percent a year, which is somewhat less than the average variability of Zenith and AT&T.

This example illustrates an important general point. As long as stock prices do not move exactly together, the risk of a diversified portfolio will be less than the average risk of the separate holdings. Portfolio risk, therefore, depends not only on the risk of the individual stocks but on the degree of correlation between the stocks.

The Trade-Off between Risk and Return

The crosses in Figure 6.2 describe the prospects for two hypothetical stocks. Stock A is expected to offer the higher return, but stock B has the attraction of lower risk. Thus, as portfolio manager, you face a trade-off between expected return and risk.

Instead of investing everything in stock A or B, you could put a proportion of the money in each. The dotted line in Figure 6.2 shows what would happen if you did so. The expected return on the portfolio would simply be a weighted average of the expected returns on the individual stocks. But thanks to the magical power of diversification, the risk of the portfolio would be less than the average risk of the individual holdings. The lower the correlation between the returns on the two stocks, the more you could reduce your risk by diversification.

Figure 6.3 shows how portfolio choice is enlarged when you can select from a large number of stocks. Each cross shows the expected return and risk of an individual stock. By holding these stocks in different proportions, you can obtain any of the combinations of risk and expected return within the shaded area. In each case the effect of holding a portfolio of stocks is to reduce risk.

Most investors prefer portfolios that offer the highest expected return for a given risk. Such portfolios are known as

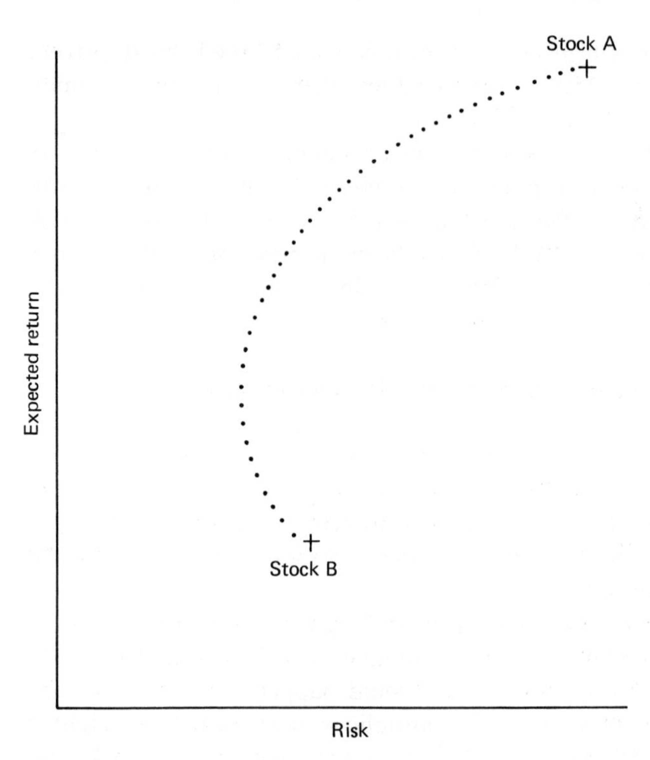

Figure 6.2
By holding stocks A and B in different proportions it is possible to obtain any of these combinations of risk and expected return.

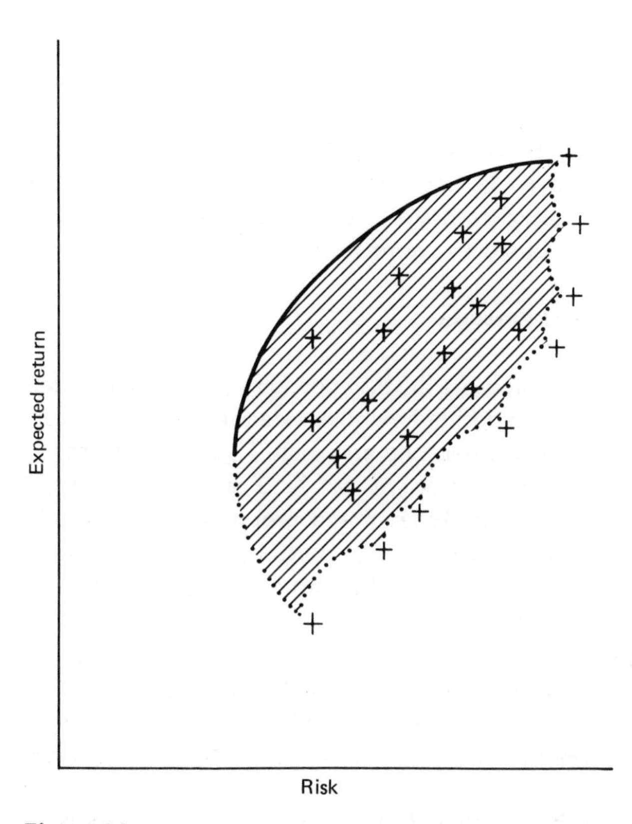

Figure 6.3
By holding different combinations of stocks it is possible to obtain any of these combinations of risk and expected return.

"efficient portfolios" and are represented by the solid line in figure 6.3. They vary from a diversified spread of stocks offering the least possible risk to the single stock offering the highest expected return. To discover these efficient portfolios, you need to know the expected return from each stock, the risk of each stock, and how closely the returns on each pair of stocks are related.[1]

The Optimal Portfolio

In addition to choosing the best portfolio of common stocks, you also need to decide how to divide the money between the common stock portfolio and cash. Figure 6.4 illustrates the choice. Suppose that you can lend cash to earn a risk-free rate of interest. By lending a proportion of the funds and investing the remainder in portfolio S, you can obtain any combination of expected return and risk shown by the solid line in figure 6.4. Suppose also that you are not only able to lend money at the risk-free interest rate but can borrow at this interest rate. In that case by borrowing to invest in portfolio S, you can achieve any combination of expected return and risk shown by the dotted line in figure 6.4.

Portfolio S is a superefficient portfolio. Any investor who wants the highest expected return for a given level of risk cannot do better than invest in S and borrow or lend the balance.[2]

How much the investor should invest in portfolio S is a matter between him and his courage. The lionhearted investor may be prepared to invest all of his wealth or more in S, whereas his more chicken-livered colleague may prefer to invest only a small proportion in S and to keep the balance in Treasury bills or a deposit account. But regardless of the investor's attitude to risk, the mix of stocks is unchanged.

Portfolio selection is made easier when the task is separated into distinct steps. The first problem is to choose the common

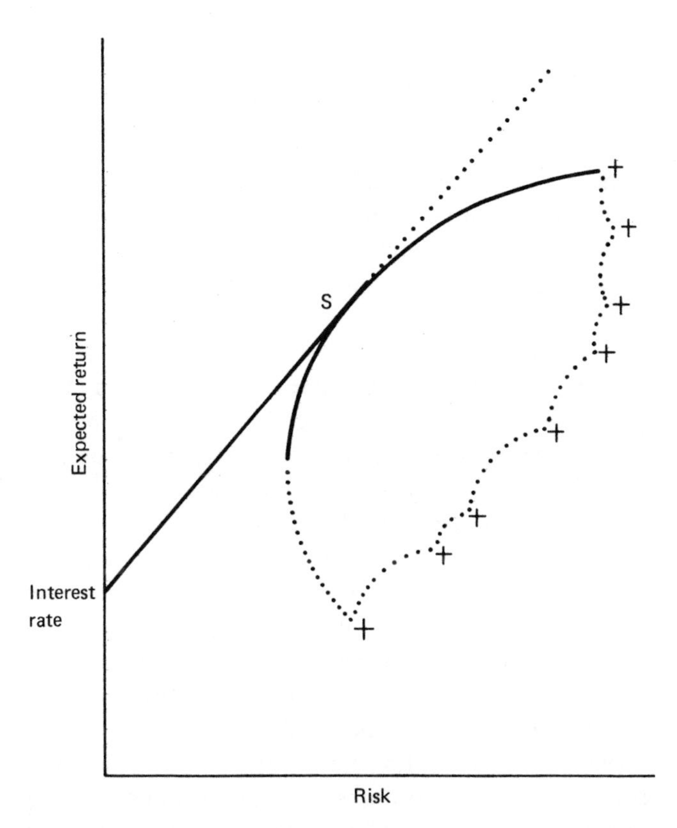

Figure 6.4
The straight line shows the combinations of risk and expected return from a mixture of stock portfolio S and risk-free borrowing or lending.

stock portfolio. Since you can earn the risk-free rate of interest by investing in a bank deposit account, you will want to buy stocks only if they offer some extra reward for taking on risk. The best stock portfolio (portfolio S) is the one that offers the highest possible ratio of expected reward to risk. Once you have identified this portfolio, you need to think about the proportion of the fund that should be invested in it. It is only at this stage that you need to consider how much risk should be taken.[3]

Which stock portfolio is best for an investor depends on the opportunities that he faces. For example, if he is taxed on dividend income, then high yielding stocks will be relatively less attractive than if he is not taxed on income. So there may be a best stock portfolio for funds that are taxed and a different one for those that are exempt.

Many brokers or investment counselors view their job as that of a financial interior decorator, skillfully designing portfolios to suit their clients' personalities. Likewise many companies entrust the management of their pension funds to a bank, but they are unwilling to allow the bank to pool their equity portfolio with that of other investors. Instead they believe that their fund needs to be tailored to their individual needs and that if it is managed separately, it will command a disproportionately large share of the manager's attention. Such companies are also guilty of the interior decorator fallacy. Funds that face the same opportunities should invest in the same equity portfolio, and they can generally be managed more effectively on a pooled basis.

Notes

1. The theory of portfolio selection owes its origins to Harry Markowitz (1). He not only demonstrated how the risk of a diversified portfolio depends on the risk of the individual stocks and the correlation between their returns, he showed how once the manager has estimated the expected return and risk of each stock and the

correlation between each pair of stocks, mathematical programming techniques can be used to find the set of efficient portfolios.

2. If you don't believe this, try drawing a line from the interest rate through a different efficient portfolio. The line will at all points lie below the one that passes through S. In other words, for any given level of risk, you could obtain a higher expected return by investing in S and borrowing or lending the balance.

3. This idea that the investor's attitude to risk should not affect the composition of the common stock portfolio was first discovered by James Tobin (2).

References

Two classics on the theory of portfolio selection:

(1) Markowitz, H. M. *Portfolio Selection: Efficient Diversification of Investments*. New York: John Wiley & Sons, 1959.

(2) Tobin, J. "Liquidity Preference as Behavior Toward Risk." *Review of Economic Studies* 25 (February 1958):65–86.

Merton's paper provides a valuable analysis of the properties of the efficient set of portfolios:

(3) Merton, R. C. "An Analytic Derivation of the Efficient Portfolio Frontier." *Journal of Financial and Quantitative Analysis* 7 (September 1972):1151–1172.

Cass and Stiglitz examine the conditions for separating portfolio selection from investor preferences:

(4) Cass, D., and Stiglitz, J. "The Structure of Investor Preferences and Asset Returns and Separability in Portfolio Allocation: A Contribution to the Pure Theory of Mutual Funds." *Journal of Economic Theory* 2 (June 1970):122–160.

7 How Stocks Move Together

Diversification reduces risk as long as stocks do not move in perfect unison. Therefore, it is important to examine how far stocks are interrelated and how far they follow their own muse.

Benefits of Diversification

One has only to observe the majestic rise and fall of the stock market index to realize that there is a pervasive market-wide influence that in some measure affects all stocks. It is this influence that limits the scope for reducing risk by diversification. No matter how well the portfolio is diversified, it remains exposed to the risk that the market as a whole will plummet and carry everything in its path.

The second column of table 7.1 shows how diversification reduces, but does not eliminate, portfolio risk. A completely undiversified portfolio would include only one stock. Typically the variability of such a portfolio would be about 40 percent a year. By contrast a fully diversified portfolio would include holdings in every stock in the market. Its variability would be about 22 percent a year. Thus, by spreading his investment as widely as possible, the investor could have reduced the portfolio's risk by almost a half.

Fortunately, it is unnecessary to hold the entire market in order to obtain most of this potential reduction in risk. For

Table 7.1
Risk of a portfolio that is evenly divided among a number of typical stocks

Number of holdings	Yearly variability %	Reduction in variability as % of potential	Yearly diversifiable variability %
1	40	0	33.5
2	32.3	43	23.7
3	29.2	60	19.3
4	27.6	69	16.8
5	26.5	75	14.9
6	25.8	78	13.6
7	25.3	81	12.7
8	24.9	83	11.9
9	24.6	85	11.2
10	24.3	87	10.5
15	23.6	91	8.8
20	23.2	93	7.7
50	22.4	97	4.7
100	22.2	98	3.6
All stocks	21.9	100	0

example, the third column of table 7.1 shows that a portfolio of ten typical stocks provides 87 percent of the possible advantages of diversification, and one of twenty such stocks provides 93 percent of the advantages.[1] This is cheering news for the private investor who does not have the means to invest in a large number of stocks. However, it may be bad news for the institutional investment manager who believes that it is possible to make superior profits by picking undervalued stocks. Unless the fund is concentrated in a relatively small number of stocks, the scope for good (or bad) performance is limited, and the portfolio's performance will be far more dependent on the movement of the market than on the manager's choice of stocks.

In table 7.1 we have relied on hypothetical portfolios to demonstrate the power and limits of diversification. In practice investors do not divide their funds evenly among so many "typical" stocks, but it nevertheless remains true that most large stock portfolios are very well diversified. For example, one study analyzed the common stock portfolios of 200 pension funds between 1971 and 1975.[2] On average 96 percent of the variability of these portfolios could be attributed to fluctuations in the general market. Like our broadly diversified portfolios in table 7.1, these pension funds had eliminated most of the potential gain from good security analysis or potential loss from poor security analysis.

Diversified Portfolios Still Deviate from the Market

The ultimate in diversification is a portfolio that holds every stock in the market. Such a portfolio has no diversifiable risk, and its return is always identical to the market return. Although fully diversified portfolios occur only in economists' dreams, we have seen that in practice only a few holdings are needed to eliminate a large part of the diversifiable risk. This would seem to imply that as long as a portfolio is reasonably diversified, its return will be almost identical to the market return. This is not so. While a large part of diversifiable risk is rapidly eliminated, the residue can still cause the portfolio's return to deviate noticeably from that of the market. The fourth column of table 7.1 shows the effects of that last bit of diversifiable risk. For example, a portfolio that is equally divided among 100 stocks will have a diversifiable risk of 3.6 percent a year. It will not be much riskier than the market, but approximately one year in three its return will differ from the market return by at least 3.6 percent. Such deviations do not offer much opportunity to make superior profits by picking undervalued stocks, but they do explain why two well-diversified stock portfolios do not always provide the same return.[3]

If you are a professional investment manager, you may feel that a decline in the value of your portfolio is less likely to attract criticism if there is a simultaneous fall in the value of everybody else's portfolio. So you may be anxious to avoid any chance that your portfolio return will differ from that of the market. By contrast, your client is unlikely to feel that universal misery is less painful than individual misery. Thus, while your focus is on minimizing the deviations between your portfolio return and the market, the client's interest is in the amount of risk that the portfolio bears. In such cases you may be tempted to hold a more widely diversified portfolio than your client would wish.

Influence of Industry Membership on Price Movements

One reason stocks move together is that they are affected by a pervasive market-wide influence. No matter how many stocks are held, the investor remains exposed to the risk of a general market decline.

The market is a "club" to which all stocks belong, but there are also more exclusive clubs that unite only particular groups of stocks. To identify these secret societies, we need to examine only that portion of the price movement that is neither peculiar to the individual stock nor due to variations in the overall market. Once we have stripped the stocks of these disguises, we can observe which ones tend to behave in a similar manner.

A classic study of this kind examined the returns of 63 NYSE stocks between 1927 and 1960.[4] Each stock belonged to one of six industry groups, based on the SEC two-digit classification. These industries were tobacco products, petroleum products, metals, railroads, utilities, and retail stores. First, an estimate was made of the returns that would have occurred if there had been no unusual market moves or events peculiar to the stock. The 63 stocks were then paired together in all possible ways. The pair with the highest correlation was Continental Oil and Atlantic Refining. Thus, after removal of the market influence and individual peculiarities, these two stocks showed the closest affinity. Continental Oil and Atlantic Refining were then added together to form a composite stock. This left 62 "stocks." These were again paired together in all possible ways. The pair on this occasion with the highest correlation was Skelly Oil and the Continental/Atlantic composite. Therefore, these three stocks were combined into a new composite stock and the whole exercise was repeated for the 61 "stocks." On each round a stock combined with another stock or with a composite stock, or two composite stocks combined.

The results of this process are illustrated in figure 7.1. On the first round (far left), Continental and Atlantic combined to form a composite stock (indicated by solid black). On round 2, they were joined by Skelly. Other oil companies joined the club until round 6, when Southern California Edison and Pacific Gas and Electric formed a separate club (represented by horizontal hatching). Notice the gradual emergence of other industry groups. By round 40, they included a group composed of the four nonferrous metal stocks. In round 53, this group merged with another formed largely of steel stocks. By round 57 the groupings corresponded exactly to the SEC two-digit classification, with the exception of Bayuk Cigar, Consolidated Cigar, and Laclede Gas, which turned traitors to their industries and aligned themselves with retail stocks.

No one told these stocks what alliances to form; they did so on the basis of mutual affinity. The interesting aspect of the study is that after allowing for individual peculiarities and the effect of the market, industry membership appears to have been the most important single influence in determining price movement.

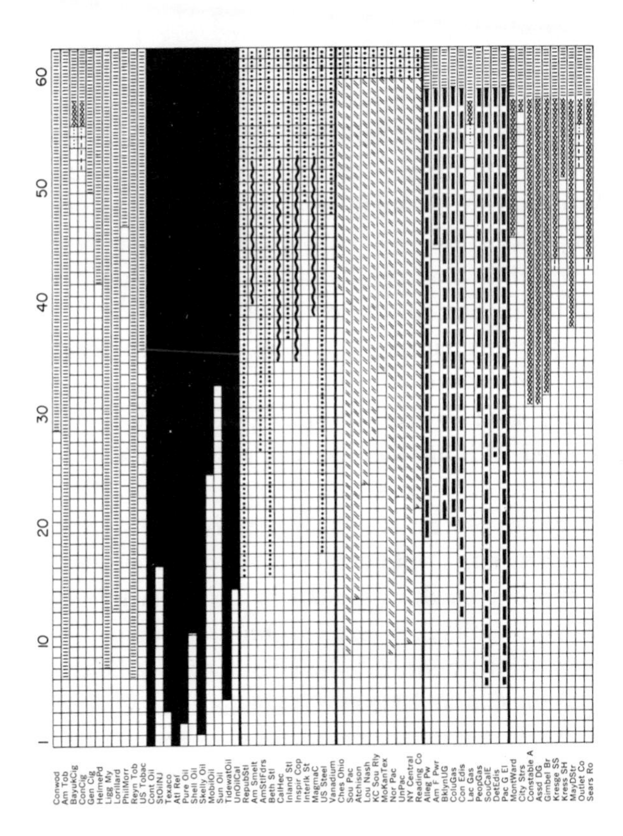

Figure 7.1
Family formations of NYSE stocks, 1927–1960. From B. F. King, "Market and Industry Factors in Stock Price Behavior," *Journal of Business* 39 (January 1966):139–190.

Factors Affecting Stock Price Performance

The performance of any stock is subject to four different influences:

A market factor that affects all stocks.

An industry factor that affects all stocks within the one industry.

A variety of other factors that affect the performance of limited groups of stocks other than industry groups.

An influence that affects only the one stock.

In the case of the 63 stocks just considered, the market factor accounted on average for 31 percent of the variability between 1952 and 1960; 12 percent of the variability was due to the industry influence; 37 percent was due to the influence of other groupings; and the remaining 20 percent of the variability was on average peculiar to the individual stock.[5]

Partly because the industry factor is so important, most research departments contain a number of industry specialists. This arrangement enables the portfolio manager to weigh the prospects for each industry and judge whether to have an above- or below-average stake in each industry. Unfortunately, while the industry factor may be the most important single influence that causes limited groups of stocks to behave alike, it is by no means the only such influence. Therefore, as long as the manager confines his attention to the prospects for industries and specific companies, he may not be aware that the portfolio's performance is heavily dependent on the level of interest rates or the value of the dollar or a rise in oil prices. In order to avoid such unpleasant surprises, the manager needs information on how his holdings are likely to be affected by factors that cut across industry lines.[6] The organization of most research departments is not well suited to providing this information.

International Diversification

Our discussion of diversification so far has focused entirely on U.S. stocks, but risk can be reduced even further by investing in foreign stock markets.

Spreading risk across a number of U.S. stocks is most effective when the fortunes of these stocks are not closely related. In the same way, international diversification is most effective when the fortunes of each country's stock markets are not closely related. Table 7.2 shows the correlation between the returns on country indexes between 1967 and 1980. Some markets tended to move more closely together than others. For example, the United States and Canadian markets were quite highly correlated, and so were the West German, Swiss, and Dutch markets. To a large extent, however, stock markets of the world march to their own idiosyncratic drums.

Figure 7.2 compares the gains from domestic and international diversification. The upper line shows that by spreading risk across a large number of U.S. stocks you can reduce the risk by about 48 percent. The lower line shows what would happen if you selected the same number of stocks randomly from eight countries.[7] You can see that a well-diversified international portfolio is only about one-third as risky as a single U.S. stock and about two-thirds as risky as a diversified portfolio of U.S. stocks.

In some cases there may be financial penalties to international diversification. For example, when you invest in a foreign equity market, you may be liable to extra taxes or costs that the local investor does not incur. Similarly, a foreign investor may be liable to extra taxes or costs when he invests in the United States. Any discrimination of this kind provides an incentive for each investor to keep a significant portion of his funds at home. But the benefits of risk spreading are so large that such financial penalties would need to exceed

Table 7.2
Correlations between stock market returns of ten countries, 1967–1980

	United States	Canada	United Kingdom	Belgium	France	Germany	Italy	Holland	Switzerland	Japan
United States	1.0									
Canada	0.7	1.0								
United Kingdom	0.5	0.5	1.0							
Belgium	0.5	0.5	0.5	1.0						
France	0.4	0.4	0.4	0.5	1.0					
Germany	0.3	0.3	0.3	0.5	0.4	1.0				
Italy	0.2	0.2	0.4	0.3	0.3	0.2	1.0			
Holland	0.3	0.2	0.1	0.5	0.2	0.5	0.1	1.0		
Switzerland	0.5	0.4	0.5	0.6	0.4	0.5	0.3	0.4	1.0	
Japan	0.3	0.2	0.2	0.3	0.1	0.3	0.2	0.3	0.3	1.0

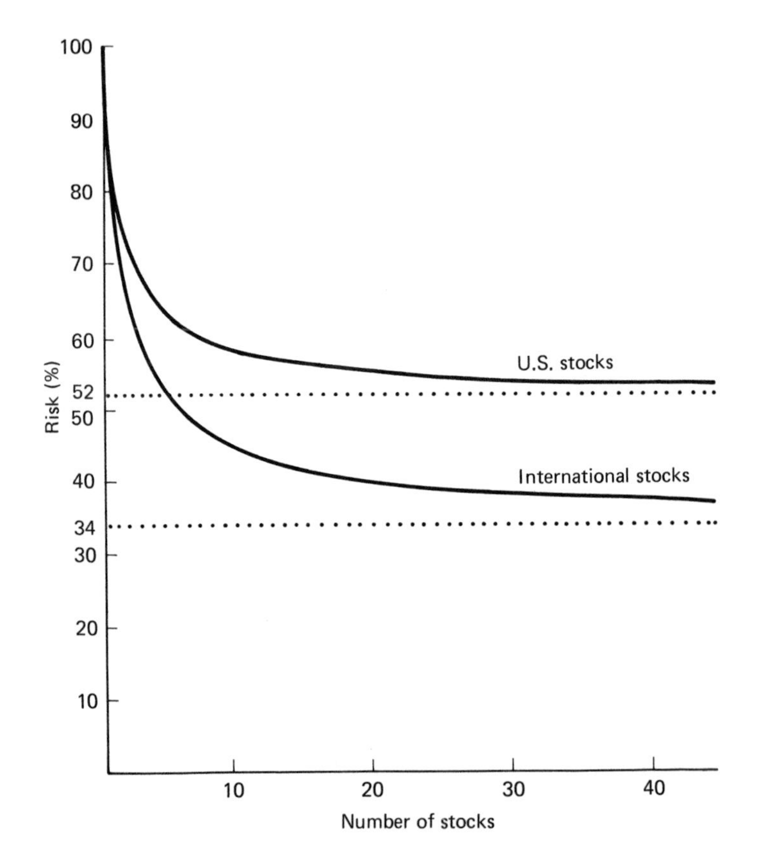

Figure 7.2
It is possible to reduce risk substantially by selecting stocks from eight countries rather than from the United States alone. From B. Solnik, "Why Not Diversify Internationally Rather than Domestically?", *Financial Analysts Journal* 30 (July–August 1974):48–54.

4 percent a year to deter investors from placing any funds overseas.[8] It is not surprising, therefore, that many U.S. investors are coming round to a view that has long been held by their continental European counterparts: You need a very positive reason *not* to invest a significant proportion of your stock portfolio overseas.

Notes

1. These figures are theoretical calculations, but several researchers have used past stock price data to show that the actual rate at which diversification reduces risk would have been very similar to the figures shown in table 7.1. See, for example, Evans and Archer (1) and Wagner and Lau (3).

2. See Beebower and Bergstrom (4).

3. This was pointed out by McDonald (2).

4. See King (8). A subsequent study by Meyers (11), which looked at a larger number of industries but fewer stocks within each industry, observed slightly weaker industry effects.

5. The importance of the market factor appears to have been declining over the past half-century, and there is some evidence that it is now weaker than it was in the 1952–1960 period. See, for example, Fama (13), pp. 128–131.

6. An interesting paper by Treynor (12) observed that stocks are primarily vehicles for participating in factors and argued that the principal task of the security analyst is to describe how each stock is likely to be affected by these factors.

7. See Solnik (25).

8. See Cooper and Lessard (16).

References

Some studies of the effect of diversification on risk:

(1) Evans, J. L., and Archer, S. H. "Diversification and the Reduction of Dispersion: An Empirical Analysis." *Journal of Finance* 23 (December 1968):761–767.

(2) McDonald, J. G. "Diversification and Exposure to Risk." *Financial Analysts Journal* 31 (March–April 1975):42–50.

(3) Wagner, W. H., and Lau, S. C. "The Effect of Diversification on Risk." *Financial Analysts Journal* 27 (November–December 1971):48–53.

This paper provides an example of how well institutional portfolios are diversified:

(4) Beebower, G. L., and Bergstrom, G. L. "A Performance Analysis of Pension and Profit Sharing Portfolios: 1966–1975." *Financial Analysts Journal* 33 (May–June 1977):31–42.

Some studies of the relationships between stocks and the implications for managers:

(5) Elton, E. J., and Gruber, M. J. "Estimating the Dependence Structure of Share Prices—Implications for Portfolio Selection." *Journal of Finance* 28 (December 1973):1203–1232.

(6) Farrell, J. L., Jr. "Homogeneous Stock Groupings: Implications for Portfolio Management." *Financial Analysts Journal* 31 (May–June 1975):50–62.

(7) Fertuck, L. "A Test of Industry Indices Based on SIC Codes." *Journal of Financial and Quantitative Analysis* 10 (December 1975):837–848.

(8) King, B. F. "Market and Industry Factors in Stock Price Behavior." *Journal of Business* 39 (January 1966):139–190.

(9) Livingston, M. "Industry Movements of Common Stocks." *Journal of Finance* 32 (June 1977):861–874.

(10) Martin, J. D., and Klemkosky, R. C. "The Effect of Homogeneous Stock Groupings on Portfolio Risk." *Journal of Business* 49 (July 1976):339–349.

(11) Meyers, S. L. "A Re-examination of Market and Industry Factors in Stock Price Behavior." *Journal of Finance* 28 (June 1973):695–705.

(12) Treynor, J. L. "The Coming Revolution in Investment Management." In J. L. Bicksler, ed., *Methodology in Finance—Investments.* Lexington, Mass.: Lexington Books, D. C. Heath, 1972.

Fama's book includes the suggestion that the market influence has been weaker in recent years:

(13) Fama, E. F. *Foundations of Finance.* New York: Basic Books, 1976.

Some studies of the case for international diversification:

(14) Agmon, T. B. "The Relations among Equity Markets—A Study of Share Price Co-movements in the United States, United Kingdom, Germany and Japan." *Journal of Finance* 27 (September 1972):839–856.

(15) Bergstrom G. L. "A New Route to Higher Returns and Lower Risk." *Journal of Portfolio Management* 2 (Fall 1975):30–38.

(16) Cooper, I. A., and Lessard, D. R. "International Capital Market Equilibrium with Deadweight Costs to Foreign Investment." Unpublished paper, 1981.

(17) Grubel, H. G. "Internationally Diversified Portfolios." *American Economic Review* 58 (December 1968):1299–1314.

(18) Grubel, H. G., and Fadner, K. "The Interdependence of International Equity Markets." *Journal of Finance* 26 (March 1971):89–94.

(19) Hilliard, J. E. "The Relationship between Equity Indices on World Exchanges." *Journal of Finance* 34 (March 1979):103–114.

(20) Lessard, D. R. "International Portfolio Diversification: Multivariate Analysis for a Group of Latin American Countries." *Journal of Finance* 28 (June 1973):619–633.

(21) Lessard, D. R. "World, Country and Industry Relationships in Equity Returns: Implications for Risk Reduction through International Diversification." *Financial Analysts Journal* 32 (January–February 1976):32–38.

(22) Levy, H., and Sarnat, M. "International Diversification of Investment Portfolios." *American Economic Review* 60 (September 1970):668–675.

(23) Panton, D., Lesseg, V., and Joy, O. "Comovement of International Equity Markets: A Taxonomic Approach." *Journal of Financial and Quantitative Analysis* 11 (September 1976):415–432.

(24) Ripley, D. "Systematic Elements in the Linkage of National Stock Market Indices." *Review of Economics and Statistics* 55 (August 1973):356–361.

(25) Solnik, B. "Why Not Diversify Internationally Rather than Domestically?" *Financial Analysts Journal* 30 (July–August 1974):48–54.

8 The Effect of the Market on Stock Prices

We have seen that a stock's variability stems from movements in the overall market; industry-wide factors; factors that are common to other limited groups of stocks; and factors specific to the individual stock. For an investor who holds only one stock, the last three sources of variability loom large, but as the number of stocks in the portfolio increases, these risks are progressively diversified away. For a well-diversified portfolio, almost all the variability results from fluctuations in the overall market.

Investment managers are aware that fluctuations in the market do not affect all stocks equally. They talk about aggressive stocks that respond sharply to market changes and defensive stocks that are largely immune to market changes. They know that a portfolio of aggressive stocks is more risky than the market as a whole and that a portfolio of defensive stocks is less risky.

Because the risk of a diversified portfolio depends predominantly on whether it is invested in aggressive or defensive stocks, investment managers have been concerned with quantifying these differences. The most common yardstick of aggressiveness is known as "beta." Beta measures the sensitivity of the stock price to changes in the market. Stocks with a beta greater than 1 are aggressive stocks; they respond sharply to market changes. For example, if a stock has a beta of 2.0, an extra 1 percent change in the market will bring about an extra 2 percent change in the price of the stock. A well-diversified portfolio of such stocks would, therefore, be twice as variable as the market.

Stocks with a beta less than 1 are defensive stocks; they are largely unaffected by market fluctuations. For example, if a stock has a beta of 0.5, an extra 1 percent change in the market will bring about an extra 0.5 percent change in the price of the stock. A well-diversified portfolio of such stocks would be half as variable as the market.

Of course, on average stocks have a beta of 1.0; an extra 1 percent change in the market brings about a 1 percent change in stock prices. A well-diversified portfolio of average stocks would have the same variability as the market index.

Estimating Beta

To determine which are the aggressive and defensive stocks, a useful first step is to estimate how they have been affected by market fluctuations in the past. Figure 8.1 shows how this can be done. Each cross in this figure depicts the return on Zenith stock and the return on the market index in a different three-month period. For example, the circled cross shows that in one three-month period (the first quarter of 1976) Zenith's stock price rose by 54 percent, whereas the market index rose by only 13 percent. Notice that more often than not Zenith stock outperformed the market when the index rose and underperformed the market when the index fell. Thus Zenith stock behaved like an aggressive stock.

To measure more precisely the sensitivity of Zenith's stock price to fluctuations in the market, we can draw a line of best fit through the crosses in figure 8.1. The gradient of this line is 2.6. In other words, on average an extra 1 percent change in the index resulted in an extra 2.6 percent change in Zenith's stock price. On past evidence, therefore, we would judge that Zenith has a beta of 2.6.

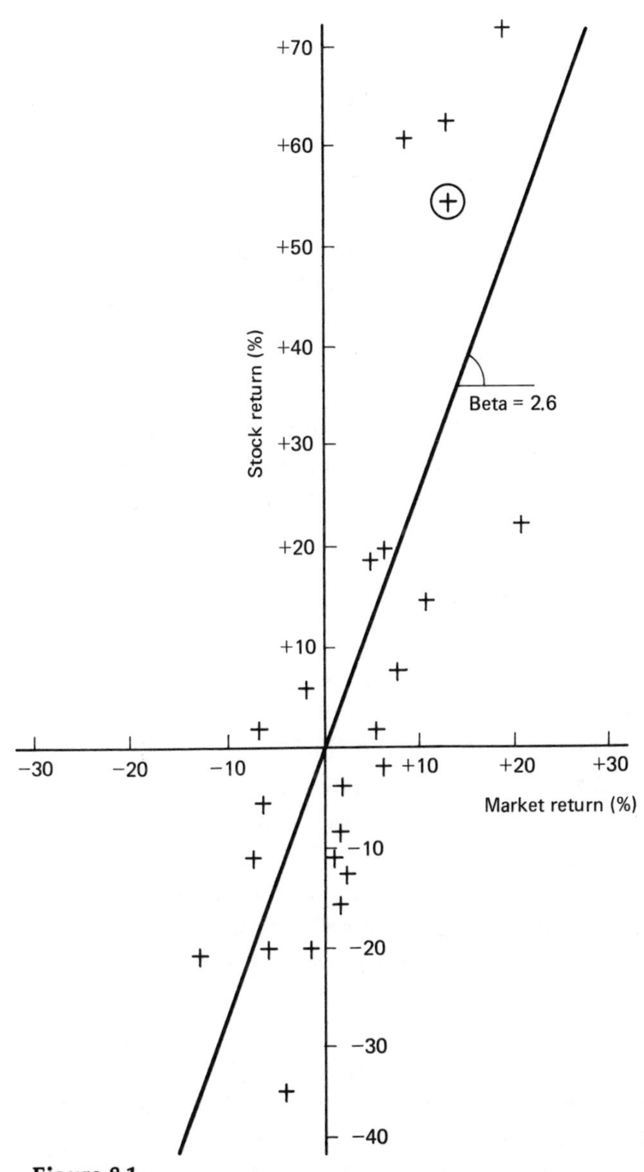

Figure 8.1
Scatter diagram of quarterly returns from Zenith and from the market index, 1975–1980.

Figure 8.2 is a scatter diagram of the quarterly returns on AT&T's stock and the market index. In contrast to Zenith, AT&T seems to have behaved like a defensive stock. It performed worse than the market when the index rose and performed better when the index fell. The slope of the line of best fit shows that on average an extra 1 percent change in the index resulted in an extra 0.3 change in the price of AT&T's stock. In other words, AT&T has a beta of 0.3.

In chapter 6 we saw that on past evidence Zenith is a much more variable stock than AT&T. So it would be far riskier to invest all your money in Zenith than in AT&T. Figures 8.1 and 8.2 tell us that Zenith also has a higher beta than AT&T. Thus it is not only a riskier investment if held in isolation, it also has a much greater effect on the risk of a diversified portfolio.

Notice that with each of our stocks there was a wide scatter about the line of best fit. Sometimes the return was substantially higher than would have been expected on the basis of the market's performance, and at other times it was substantially worse. This is simply a reminder that only a small proportion of the variation in the price of an individual stock is due to fluctuations in the overall market; the greater part is due to news that is specific to the particular stock or to limited groups of stocks.

As stocks are aggregated into portfolios, this nonmarket variability is progressively diversified away, and the variability that stems from the market becomes the dominant source of risk. You can see this from figures 8.3 and 8.4, which show the annual returns from a high-beta mutual fund and a low-beta fund, respectively. The crosses in each figure cluster closely around the fitted line. Thus each mutual fund has diversified away much of the nonmarket variability, and the remaining risk comes largely from fluctuations in the market. Since a market change has almost twice the

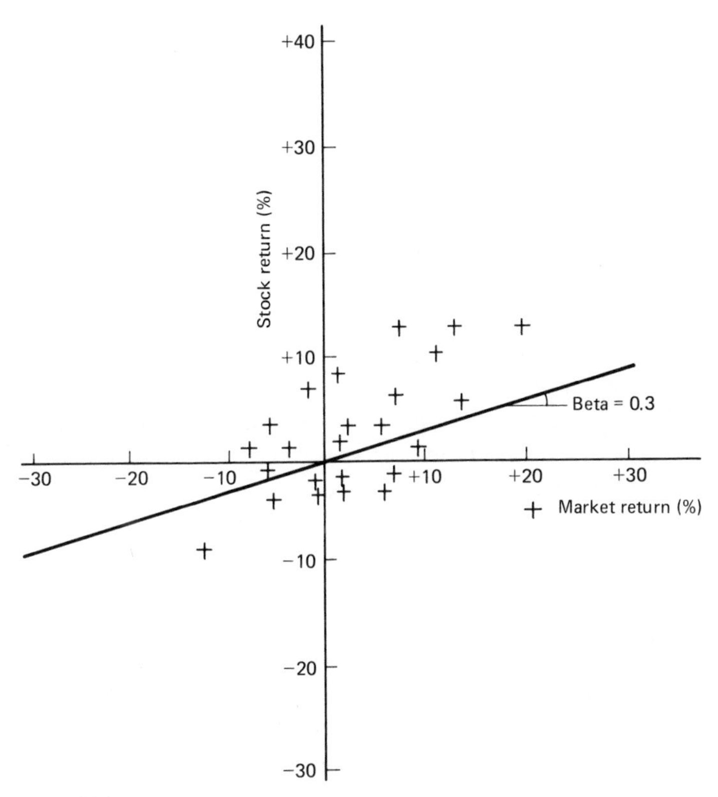

Figure 8.2
Scatter diagram of quarterly returns from AT&T and from the market index, 1975–1980.

effect on Keystone S-4 Fund as on Keystone S-1 Fund, the variability of Keystone S-4 is almost twice that of S-1.

Do Past Betas Foretell Future Betas?

Although we can now measure the extent to which a stock has been affected by market movements in the past, investors are more interested in the future than the past. They would like to know whether a stock's past sensitivity to market movements provides any guide to future behavior.

Suppose that you estimated the sensitivity of each of the NYSE stocks to market movements during the previous five years and then divided the stocks into ten groups, from those with the lowest betas (group 1) to those with the highest betas (group 10). Five years later you repeated the exercise and measured the proportion of the surviving stocks that were still in the same group as before. Table 8.1 shows what you would have found. For example, you can see that 41 percent of the stocks that you had placed in group 10 would still have been there five years later and 64 percent of them would have been in groups 9 or 10. Clearly, estimates of beta based on past data do tell you something about how a stock is likely to be affected by future market movements.[1]

Are these predictable differences in beta worth bothering about? To answer that question, we can divide stocks into several groups on the basis of their estimated beta in some past period and calculate the average beta for each group of stocks in the subsequent period. You can see from table 8.2 that the stocks that you thought had the lowest betas were not quite as insensitive to market changes as you believed. And the stocks that you thought had the highest betas were not as sensitive to market changes as you believed. Nevertheless in each period the stocks in the first group were substantially less affected by market fluctuations than those in the last group.[2]

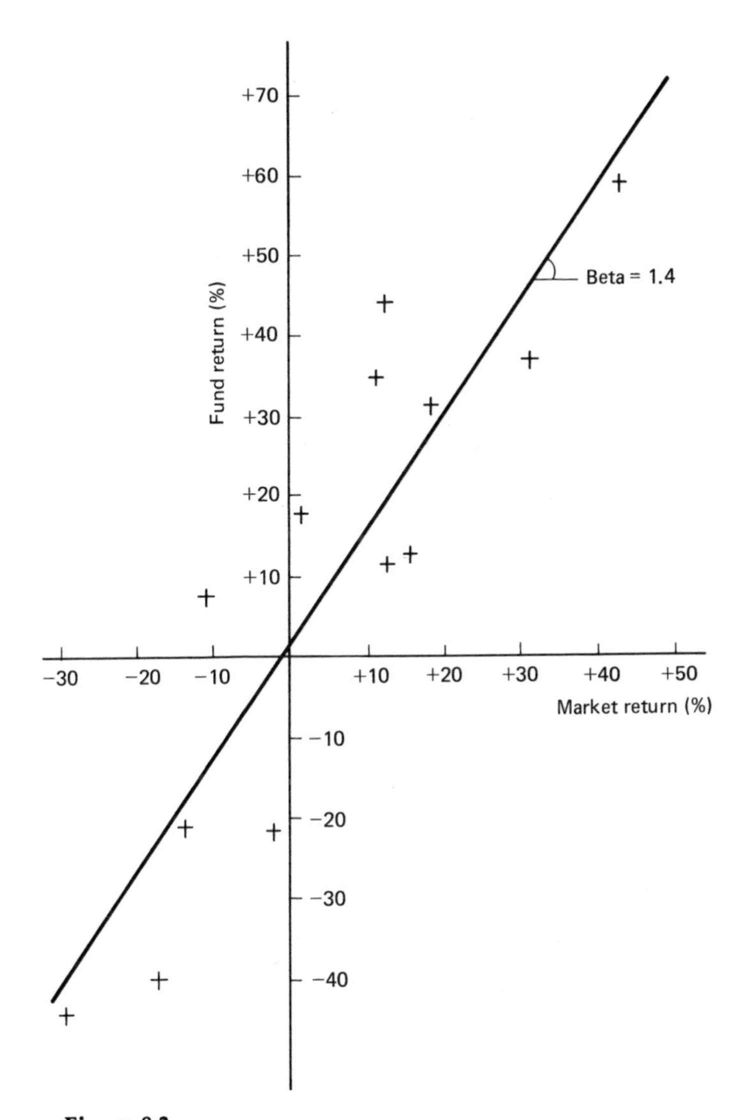

Figure 8.3
Scatter diagram of annual returns from Keystone S-4 Fund and from market index, 1968–1980.

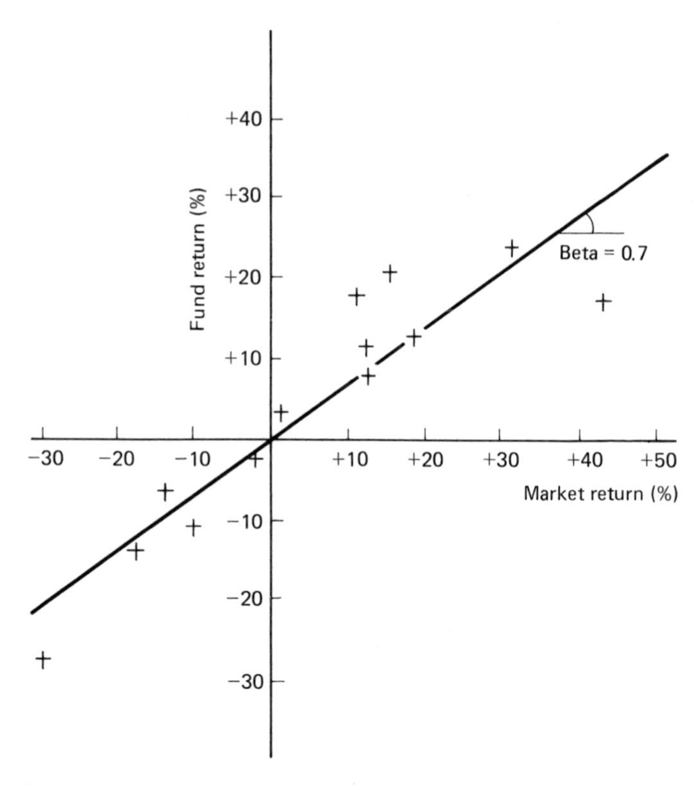

Figure 8.4
Scatter diagram of annual returns from Keystone S-1 Fund and from market index, 1968–1980.

Table 8.1
Percentage of NYSE stocks in each beta group in successive five-year periods, 1931–1967

Beta group in first five years	Beta group in second five years									
	10	9	8	7	6	5	4	3	2	1
10	41	23	14	7	6	4	2	1	1	1
9	23	21	17	14	9	7	5	3	1	1
8	14	17	18	14	11	10	7	4	2	2
7	9	14	17	14	13	12	10	6	3	2
6	6	11	12	14	15	13	12	9	5	3
5	4	7	9	11	15	15	16	12	8	4
4	4	5	8	11	12	13	14	16	11	7
3	2	3	5	8	10	12	14	17	17	12
2	1	2	3	4	5	8	12	17	23	25
1	0	1	1	2	3	5	8	12	24	44

Source: W. F. Sharpe and G. M. Cooper, "Risk-Return Classes of New York Stock Exchange Stocks, 1931–1967," *Financial Analysts Journal* 28 (March–April 1972):46–54.

Good Betas and Bad Betas

Estimating betas may sound simple, but in practice there are a number of tricks to obtaining good estimates. For example, if a stock went up or down more than the market yesterday, you would not necessarily conclude that the price change was a consequence of the market movement. In order to be confident that the stock price really was sensitive to market fluctuations, you would need to observe its behavior on a number of separate occasions.

To obtain a representative sample of price changes, you need a long price history. But the longer you look back, the more likely that the company's beta may have changed. So, when estimating betas, you are faced with a trade-off be-

Table 8.2
Average beta of stocks grouped by beta in first seven-year period

	Average beta		Average beta		Average beta		Average beta		Average beta	
Portfolio	7/26 to 6/33	7/33 to 6/40	7/33 to 6/40	7/40 to 6/47	7/40 to 6/47	7/47 to 6/54	7/47 to 6/54	7/54 to 6/61	7/54 to 6/61	7/61 to 6/68
1	0.5	0.6	0.4	0.6	0.4	0.6	0.4	0.6	0.4	0.6
2	0.9	1.0	0.7	0.8	0.6	0.8	0.7	0.7	0.6	0.7
3	1.2	1.3	0.9	0.9	0.7	0.9	0.8	1.0	0.8	0.9
4			1.2	1.1	0.9	1.0	1.0	1.0	1.0	0.9
5			1.4	1.4	1.0	1.1	1.1	1.1	1.1	1.0
6					1.3	1.3	1.2	1.2	1.3	1.2

Source: M. E. Blume, "On the Assessment of Risk," *Journal of Finance* 26 (March 1971):1–10.

tween insufficient data and out-of-date data. A common compromise is to use a five-year price history.

If a stock is rarely traded, it is difficult to ensure that the price changes and the market changes are for the same period. These errors may not matter much if you are looking at monthly data, but they may be serious if you work with daily data. In the latter case rarely traded stocks will appear to be particularly insensitive to market changes and actively traded stocks particularly sensitive.[3]

If a stock appears to have been very sensitive to market movements in the past, there is some evidence that it has a high beta. It is possible, however, that the effect could have been a coincidence. So your best forecast is that the stock's beta is not quite as high as it appears. Similarly, if a stock appears to have been very insensitive to market movements in the past, your best forecast is that its beta is not quite as low as it appears. That is why in table 8.2 the betas turned out to be closer to 1 than past evidence seemed at first to suggest.[4]

There are good reasons why some stocks are more aggressive than others. Aggressive stocks tend to be associated with high growth companies that have cyclical revenues, heavy fixed costs, and high financial leverage. Defensive stocks tend to be associated with more mature, unlevered firms in stable or regulated industries. Thus there is a relationship between a stock's beta and the firm's accounting data. If you can measure this relationship sufficiently accurately, you may be able to obtain better estimates of beta than if you looked only at the stock's past price behavior. On the other hand, there is a danger that you may incorrectly estimate the relationship and your estimates of beta may be worse than if you ignored the accounting data entirely.[5]

Is Beta Always the Correct Measure of Risk?

The risk to you of any investment depends on the sensitivity of that investment to changes in the value of your portfolio. In other words, if you wish to measure the effect on your portfolio's risk of increasing your holding in a particular stock, then you should look at the beta of that stock measured relative to your portfolio. If that beta is greater than 1, the stock will increase portfolio risk; if it is less than 1, the stock will decrease portfolio risk.

Now it would be extremely inconvenient if we could never talk about a stock being risky without having somebody ask "To whom?" It would be equally inconvenient if each portfolio manager needed a set of betas that was calculated relative to his particular portfolio. Fortunately most large portfolios are well diversified and move closely with the market index. That is why most portfolio managers find that the beta of a stock relative to the market index provides a good measure of how much risk that stock will contribute to their portfolio.[6]

It is important, however, to look out for exceptions. If your portfolio is invested entirely in airline stocks or in Japanese stocks, it will not move closely with the U.S. market index, and the beta of any stock relative to that index will not measure the risk of that investment to you.[7]

If your portfolio does not resemble the market index, a stock's beta will not measure its effect on the risk of your portfolio. However, that does not mean you should not be interested in beta. If the market is the predominant reason that stocks move together, you will need to know how much variability arises from market movements (beta) and how much can potentially be diversified away. In the next chapter we shall look at how to construct a portfolio that gives a sensible balance between these two types of risk.

Notes

1. See Sharpe and Cooper (14).

2. See Blume (4).

3. For a discussion of the effect of thin trading on beta estimates and how to deal with the problem, see Dimson (5) and Scholes and Williams (12).

4.This means that when forecasting betas, you need to squash your estimates toward 1. For example, our best forecast of Zenith's beta would be less than 2.6, and our best forecast of AT&T's beta would be more than 0.3. For a discussion of how to adjust estimates of beta, see Blume (3) and Vasicek (15).

5. A useful review of accounting measures of risk is contained in Foster (18).

6. The beta of a stock relative to a well-diversified portfolio is equal to its beta relative to the market index divided by the beta of the portfolio relative to the market index.

7. The importance of measuring beta against the correct index has been stressed by Roll (23).

References

These papers provide evidence on the stability of betas and discuss alternative methods of estimation:

(1) Alexander, G. J., and Chervany, N. L. "On the Estimation and Stability of Beta." *Journal of Financial and Quantitative Analysis* 15 (March 1980):123–137.

(2) Altman, E. K., Jacquillat, B., and Levasseur, M. "Comparative Analysis of Risk Measures: France and the United States." *Journal of Finance* 29 (December 1974):1495–1511.

(3) Blume, M. E. "Betas and Their Regression Tendencies." *Journal of Finance* 30 (June 1975):785–796.

(4) Blume, M. E. "On the Assessment of Risk." *Journal of Finance* 26 (March 1971):1–10.

(5) Dimson, E. "Risk Measurement When Shares are Subject to Infrequent Trading." *Journal of Financial Economics* 7 (June 1979):197–226.

(6) Dimson, E., and Marsh, P. R. "The Stability of UK Risk Measures and the Problem of Thin Trading." *Journal of Finance*, forthcoming.

(7) Eubank, A. A., Jr., and Zumwalt, J. K. "An Analysis of the Forecast Error Impact of Alternative Beta Adjustment Techniques and Risk Classes." *Journal of Finance* 34 (June 1979):761–776.

(8) Fisher, L., and Kamin, J. "Good Betas and Bad Betas." Unpublished paper, Center for Research into Security Prices, University of Chicago, November 1971.

(9) Jacob, N. "The Measurement of Systematic Risk for Securities and Portfolios: Some Empirical Results." *Journal of Financial and Quantitative Analysis* 6 (March 1971):815–834.

(10) Klemkosky, R. C., and Martin, J. D. "The Adjustment of Beta Forecasts." *Journal of Finance* 30 (September 1975):1123–1128.

(11) Kon, S. J., and Lau, W. P. "Specification Tests for Portfolio Regression Parameter Stationarity and the Implications for Empirical Research." *Journal of Finance* 34 (May 1979):451–465.

(12) Scholes, M., and Williams, J. "Estimating Betas from Nonsynchronous Data." *Journal of Financial Economics* 5 (December 1977):309–328.

(13) Sharpe, W. F. "The Capital Asset Pricing Model: A 'Multi-Beta' Interpretation." In Levy, H., and Sarnat, M., eds., *Financial Decision Making Under Uncertainty*. New York: Academic Press, 1977.

(14) Sharpe, W. F., and Cooper, G. M. "Risk-Return Classes of New York Stock Exchange Stocks, 1931–1967." *Financial Analysts Journal* 28 (March–April 1972):46–54.

(15) Vasicek, O. A. "A Note on Using Cross-Sectional Information in Bayesian Estimation of Security Betas." *Journal of Finance* 28 (December 1973):1233–1239.

These studies discuss the use of accounting data to estimate risk:

(16) Beaver, W., Kettler, P., and Scholes, M. "The Association between Market-Determined and Accounting-Determined Risk Measures." *Accounting Review* 45 (October 1970):654–682.

(17) Beaver, W., and Manegold, J. "The Association between Market-Determined and Accounting-Determined Measures of Systematic

Risk: Some Further Evidence." *Journal of Financial and Quantitative Analysis* 10 (June 1975):231–284.

(18) Foster, G. *Financial Statement Analysis.* Englewood Cliffs, N. J.: Prentice-Hall, 1978.

(19) Gonedes, N. J. "Evidence on the Information Content of Accounting Numbers: Accounting-Based and Market-Based Estimates of Systematic Risk." *Journal of Financial and Quantitative Analysis* 8 (June 1973):407–444.

(20) Rosenberg, B. "Extra Market Components of Covariance among Security Prices." *Journal of Financial and Quantitative Analysis* 9 (March 1974):263–294.

(21) Rosenberg, B., and Guy, J. "Beta and Investment Fundamentals." *Financial Analysts Journal* 32 (May–June 1976):60–72, and 32 (July–August 1976):62–70.

(22) Rosenberg, B., and McKibben, W. "The Prediction of Systematic and Specific Risk in Common Stocks." *Journal of Financial and Quantitative Analysis* 8 (March 1973):312–334.

Roll's paper contains a theoretical discussion of the importance of choosing the appropriate market measure:

(23) Roll, R. "A Critique of the Asset Pricing Theory's Tests; Part 1: On Past and Potential Testability of the Theory." *Journal of Financial Economics* 4 (March 1977):129–176.

9 Passive and Active Portfolios

Investment managers often refer to passive and active portfolios. A passive portfolio is one that you would hold if you had no forecasting ability. An active portfolio consists of a series of bets on the prospects for specific stocks that seem to be mispriced.[1]

Unless you have some reason to suppose that some stocks are consistently better suited to you than others, the passive portfolio should contain an investment in the total market. But not all investors would regard the market as a sensible passive portfolio. For example, millionaires may find that stocks with a high dividend yield are likely to give a lower return after taxes than stocks with a low yield. For a millionaire, then, the passive portfolio should consist of a well-diversified portfolio with above-average weightings in stocks with low dividend yields. On the other hand, pension funds are tax-exempt and, therefore, are best placed to hold stocks with high dividend yields. The best passive strategy for a pension fund may be to hold a well-diversified portfolio with above-average weightings in stocks with high dividend yields.[2]

Most common stock portfolios effectively have a passive and an active element. In other words, they contain a core portfolio that is well diversified and seldom changed. In addition, they include above- or below-average weightings in a few stocks that offer unusually good or bad prospects.

Different Sources of Reward and Risk

The notion that we can decompose a stock portfolio into passive and active portions stems from the idea that the return on an individual stock can likewise be divided into separate parts.

Unlike Treasury bills, common stocks are risky. Therefore, any extra return from common stock is a reward for taking risk. Generally the reward will be positive, but sometimes it may be negative. There are two reasons that you may forecast a positive or negative reward for taking risk. First, you may expect a move in the overall market that will carry your stock along with it. If the stock has a high beta, it will be particularly affected by such a market move; if it has a low beta, it will be relatively unaffected. Second, your analysis of a particular stock may lead you to expect a specific reward that is over and above the reward stemming from a general market move. Half the time your forecast of the specific reward is likely to be positive and half the time it is likely to be negative.

There also are two sources of risk. First, there is the risk that you may have misjudged the outlook for the market as a whole and that your stock may plummet with the rest. Second, even if you are confident about the outlook for the market, there remains the risk that you may have incorrectly estimated the prospects for that specific stock.

Two Steps of Portfolio Management

Let us suppose for a while that stocks are related only by their common membership in the market. Thus, there is nothing that unites limited groups of stocks, such as being in the same industry or in the same geographical area. In these circumstances, whenever you buy a common stock, you are effectively making two investments: you are betting on the prospects for the specific stock and you are betting on the prospects for the market as a whole.[3] Since the returns on these investments are unrelated, the equity manager's job consists of two, logically distinct steps. First, he must construct an active portfolio consisting of a series of bets on the outlook for specific stocks. Second, he must blend in the passive porfolio so as to give the appropriate exposure to the overall market.

Step 1: The Active Portfolio

Construction of the active portfolio capitalizes on your ability to pick stocks. You should, therefore, take a long position in each stock that is expected to provide a positive specific reward and a short position in each stock that is expected to provide a negative specific reward.[4]

The active portfolio should offer the highest possible ratio of expected specific reward to specific risk. To ensure this, your holding in each stock should be directly proportional to the ratio of its expected specific reward to specific risk squared.

Suppose, for example, that you are equally optimistic about the prospects for the General Foods and United Airlines. On past evidence, UAL's specific risk is twice that of General Foods's. Since the cost of a misjudgment is greater for UAL, you should invest a smaller sum in it. But how much smaller? The proportionality rule provides the answer. Because UAL's specific risk squared is four times General Foods's specific risk squared, the active portfolio's investment in UAL should be a quarter as large as its investment in General Foods.

To construct the active portfolio you need only two items of information for each stock: its specific risk and its expected specific reward. Although past history may offer some guide to the specific risk, the forecasts of specific reward can come only from the analyst. Many investment companies do not ask their analysts for forecasts of the specific reward. For example, some require the analysts to predict the total return. Since the total return depends partly on the movement of the market, such a forecast offers no guidance as to whether you should be betting on the outlook for the market or for the specific stock. In other investment companies the analyst is required simply to recommend a purchase or sale. The proportion that should be invested in a particular stock, however, depends on the outlook for all other stocks. Therefore, the analyst is not in a position to make purchase or sale recommendations, and these recommendations do not enable you to construct the active portfolio.

If you want to measure the value of an analyst's forecasts, you should look at the number of stocks that he examines and the accuracy of his forecasts. Both are of roughly equal importance. If the analyst halves the number of stocks that he studies, he needs at least to double the proportion of the specific risk that his forecasts can explain.

Step 2: The Passive Portfolio

When you construct the active portfolio, you can forget about the outlook for the market as a whole and concentrate on the prospects for the specific stocks. Although the stocks that you buy and sell are likely to be affected by the market, they are unlikely to provide you with the stake in the market that you need. Therefore, once you have placed your bets on specific stocks, your next step is to adjust the portfolio's exposure to market movements.

This is done by buying or selling the passive portfolio. Since it is unnecessary to hold every stock in the market in order to be very well diversified, many managers find it convenient to adjust their market exposure by investing in an index fund, which is simply a well-diversified portfolio that moves closely with the market.

Some of the stocks in the passive portfolio will have positive expected specific rewards and will therefore also be held in the active portfolio. As a result, the overall fund will hold more in these stocks than if you had no forecasting ability. Other stocks will have negative expected specific rewards, and the active portfolio will contain short positions in these stocks. The overall fund may still have a net investment in these stocks, but it will be less than if you had no forecasting ability. Thus the neutral stance is to hold the stock in the same proportions as the passive portfolio. That is why it makes sense when you review your portfolio to focus on whether your weightings in each stock are above or below those in the passive portfolio.

The market is just like one more security, and you should therefore devote the same effort to forecasting market movements as you spend analyzing one stock. Similarly, you should require your investment in the passive portfolio to work as hard for you as your investments in the specific stocks. For example, if the ratio of expected reward to risk squared is ten times greater for the market than for a specific stock, then you should buy or sell the passive portfolio until your stake in the market is ten times your stake in that specific stock.

The more optimistic you are about market prospects, the more money you should invest in the passive portfolio and the less you should bet on the prospects for specific stocks. Therefore, when market prospects are bright or conditions settled, your fund should be well diversified and have a low rate of turnover. By contrast, when market prospects are poor or very uncertain, you should be more selective and active.[5]

Since investors need some inducement to take on the risk of common stock investment, the return on the market will usually be higher than the return on Treasury bills. You know that approximately half the stocks will outperform the market and the other half will underperform, but unless you have some advance knowledge as to which ones are which, you can only assume that the expected specific reward for each stock is zero. This implies that for an investor with no forecasting skill, the market is the only investment offering a positive expected reward for risk. Therefore, such an investor should invest all his money in the passive portfolio.

Most managers believe that they do have some forecasting ability that will allow them to obtain superior performance, but it is striking how little faith they then place in this ability. For example, we saw in chapter 7 that on average 96 percent of the variation in pension fund returns is due to variations in the market. This means that the typical pension fund manager is placing very limited bets on the prospects for specific stocks. If the research department analyzes 100 stocks, you should be placing such small bets on its predictions only if the correlation between the forecast and actual specific returns is about .01. If you believe that the correlation is higher than this figure, then you should be placing larger bets on the prospects for individual stocks.

Cash-Equity Split

When you construct a common stock portfolio, your aim should be to maximize the ratio of expected reward to risk. Once you have chosen the portfolio, you need to consider how much risk you are prepared to take. The fainthearted investor may wish to invest only a small proportion of his money in the common stock portfolio and leave the remainder in the bank. By contrast, the more spirited investor may even be prepared to borrow in order to invest in common stocks.

When market prospects are rosy, you will want to invest more heavily in stocks than when prospects are somber. A good rule of thumb is to adjust the common stock proportion so that you maintain a constant ratio of expected reward to variability squared. For example, if you expect that next year the reward on your equity portfolio will be only half as large as usual, then you should invest only half as much as usual in common stocks and keep the remainder in the bank.[6]

The Practice of Active-Passive Management

The notion that portfolio construction can be split into distinct steps, not only assumes that the market is the sole factor that causes stocks to move together. It also ignores a number of practical complications, such as transactions costs and the limitations on short selling. Therefore, you should not look on the simple ideas in this chapter as providing a cookbook formula for managing portfolios. They can, however, help you organize the management of a portfolio.

Some companies believe that investment management is a very competitive business and that there is little point in spending large sums trying to uncover stocks with positive or negative specific rewards. Therefore, instead of seeking to outperform the market, these firms invest in a passive portfolio, such as an index fund. There is nothing magic about a particular stock market index, and many of these funds go to inordinate trouble to match the chosen index. Nevertheless, most index funds are well diversified and thus are a sensible investment for investors with no forecasting ability.

Other companies believe that superior analysis is possible and, therefore, wish to adopt a mixed active-passive strategy. They may be prepared to pay the manager a substantial fee, but they want to make sure that he earns the fee. This means that they need to monitor the portfolio to check that he is not "closet indexing"; that is, investing in a very well-diversified portfolio while pretending to provide active management.

One response to closet indexing is to divide the stock portfolio into two. One portion is given to a manager with instructions to manage it actively, and the remainder is invested in a passive portfolio, such as an index fund. This division may sound like an obvious application of the ideas presented in this chapter, with the active manager placing bets on specific stocks and the passive manager blending in the appropriate investment in the market. Unfortunately, the arrangement cannot work effectively unless the two portfolio managers cooperate with each other. One reason for this is that the passive manager does not know how much should be invested in his fund unless he also knows the opportunities available to the active manager. Second, each overvalued stock should be held short in the active portfolio and held long in the passive portfolio. If the active manager cannot sell short or persuade the passive manager to reduce his holdings, the total fund will invest too much in overvalued shares, and roughly half the value of any security analysis will be wasted.[7]

A common alternative arrangement is to split the fund between a number of managers, each of whom tries to obtain the best performance for his portion of the fund. It is often suggested that this encourages competition between managers. However, the reverse may be true. The widespread practice of split funding has substantially reduced the importance of any one client to most investment management companies and has thus helped to sooth the investment manager's anxious sleep.

The idea behind split funding is to draw on a wide range of views about each stock. In order to get the benefit of this diversity of judgment, however, each manager must be reminded that he is responsible for only a small portion of the total fund and should, therefore, be less diversified than if he is managing the entire fund. The greater the number of managers and the more varied their predictions, the less diversified each manager should be. A second problem is that if one of these managers believes a stock is undervalued and another believes it is overvalued, the first should buy it and the second should sell it short. This will result in extra transactions costs, but it will also lead to a sensible net investment in that stock. Unfortunately, managers cannot easily sell stocks short. So, unless they cooperate, the bearish information is likely to be wasted, and the investment in the stock will be too large.

A fund that is split among several managers can at best perform only as well as a fund under a single manager with access to the same pool of information. Therefore, the split can only be justified if it allows the company to draw on a wider range of expertise. Even then, unless the division is well organized and the managers are given appropriate instructions, the fund may perform worse than one with a single manager.[8] More often than not, the split fund proves to be an expensive index fund.

Profile of an Efficiently Managed Portfolio

Portfolio management is simple if you have no forecasting ability; you just buy and hold a passive portfolio, such as an index fund. Management is also simple if you have perfect foresight; you just buy the stock that is going to give the highest return. The difficulties occur when you have very limited forecasting ability.

Chapter 3 described some studies of the forecasting ability of professional analysts. Though far from conclusive, these studies suggested that the correlation between the predicted and actual returns was typically in the region of .15.

Suppose that your forecasts of the specific returns also have a correlation of .15 with the actual outcome. Table 9.1 provides an example of what a set of forty such forecasts might look like. On average the twenty stocks that you like best will perform about 4 percent better than the twenty you like least, but many of the individual forecasts will contain substantial errors.

What sort of portfolio should you choose if your forecasts resemble those in table 9.1? One way to answer the question is by simulation. In other words, we can invent an analyst who analyzes a group of forty stocks and a portfolio manager who uses the analyst's forecasts to manage an efficient portfolio. We can also instruct our hypothetical manager to take account of transaction costs and prohibit him from selling short. By repeating the experiment a sufficient number of times, we should begin to build up a general picture of an efficiently managed portfolio.

If you are despondent at the thought that professional analysts have little forecasting ability, you can take comfort in the performance of these simulated portfolios. Despite the very imperfect forecasts, the portfolios' average annual return was about 1 percent higher than the return on the market with no increase in risk.[9]

In order to achieve these gains, you would have needed to place large bets on specific stocks. For example, on average in each year, over 20 percent of the fund was concentrated in just one stock. As a result, only three-quarters of the portfolio's variability was due to fluctuations in the market return, and the remaining quarter was due to fluctuations in the return on specific stocks.

The extent to which a manager should place bets on specific stocks depends on his forecasting ability. If his forecasts are better than those in table 9.1, he should bet more heavily than our simulated portfolios on specific stocks. However, we have seen that managers generally place very small bets on specific stocks. They claim high forecasting ability but act as if they have almost none.

If the manager places large bets on specific stocks, the portfolio's performance in any single year may be substantially different from that of the market. Consequently, although our simulated portfolios had roughly the same risk as the market, there were some years in which the portfolio

Table 9.1
Forecast and actual returns with a correlation of .15

Stock	Forecast return %	Actual return %
1	2	25
2	−12	42
3	31	20
4	− 8	11
5	2	−32
6	12	− 4
7	52	− 7
8	30	52
9	−18	−15
10	2	30
11	0	54
12	27	−19
13	30	− 7
14	31	40
15	− 4	−33
16	36	24
17	−24	1
18	7	−25
19	39	− 8
20	38	38
21	− 8	44
22	12	30
23	41	−19
24	17	23
25	15	−26
26	− 2	5
27	18	29
28	36	8
29	72	35
30	2	38
31	−19	−57

Table 9.1 (continued)

32	52	34
33	33	56
34	11	7
35	−11	27
36	45	65
37	9	18
38	36	−57
39	70	6
40	14	37

performed much better than the market and others in which it performed much worse. Indeed, in one unhappy eight-year period, the average return on the simulated portfolio was more than 8 percent a year lower than the market return. This points to an important characteristic of an efficiently managed portfolio: If you wish to outperform the market, you must be prepared to underperform it, sometimes by a substantial amount. In practice, most portfolio managers would be reluctant to accept such chances of long runs of bad luck; the penalties for inferior short-run performance are such as to discourage managers from choosing the portfolio that is in the best interests of the beneficiary.

Despite the fact that switches were assumed to involve transaction costs of 5 percent, the simulated efficient portfolios turned over nearly 40 percent of their value each year. The major part of the turnover was concentrated in the two or three stocks with outstandingly good or bad prospects. To concentrate portfolio turnover in this way requires considerable self-control. The analyst who is placed in the role of a subordinate selling his wares to the portfolio manager is tempted to uncover his daily ration of "good buys," and the manager faced with a barrage of suggested purchases finds it only too easy to succumb to dealer's itch.

Table 9.2
Consistent turnover and diversification

	Turnover	
Diversification	High	Low
High	[a]	Poor forecaster
Low	Good forecaster	[a]

a. Inconsistent strategies.

Not surprisingly, the turnover rate should depend on the investor's forecasting ability. If the forecasts are better than those in table 9.1, the turnover rate should be higher than 40 percent; if the forecasts are worse, the turnover should be less. This suggests a second important characteristic of an efficiently managed portfolio: The rate of turnover should be consistent with the level of diversification. This is illustrated by table 9.2. The temptation is to choose the forbidden top left-hand box. The high level of diversification ensures that apart from the cost of transactions the portfolio's performance matches that of the market, and the high turnover demonstrates that the manager is dealing resolutely with a very competitive situation.

The portfolio that should be held and the gains that can be expected depend on the investor's forecasting ability. The consequences of misjudging the accuracy of the forecasts are illustrated in table 9.3. If the manager believes that he has no forecasting ability, he will invest only in the passive portfolio. He is thereby assured of average performance, but he may be passing up the opportunity of superior profits if he does in fact have some forecasting skill. If the manager believes that he has exceptional skill, he will place large bets on specific stocks and turn over his portfolio rapidly. If he has assessed his ability correctly, he will make superior profits. If his assessment is wrong, he will incur extra risk with

Table 9.3
The importance of knowing your own forecasting ability

How good you *think* you are	How good you are	
	Genius	Average
Genius	Above-average performance	Below-average performance
Average	Average performance	Average performance

no reward, he will incur unnecessary transaction costs, and his performance will be worse than if he had simply bought and held the market portfolio.

It is usually left to the portfolio manager to gauge how heavily he should bet on his own ability. However, few people are the best judges of their own genius. It is, therefore, foolish to suppose that one can establish a sensible management strategy without first measuring the degree of correlation between one's forecasts and the outcome or without considering the consequences of an incorrect estimate of the quality of these forecasts.

Forecasts are a sensitive flower. If you understand their limitations, you can make significant gains. But if you have an exaggerated notion of the analyst's ability or if the forecasts that you receive are distorted, you will be fortunate not to have below-average performance.[10] Good portfolio performance, therefore, depends critically on good communication between analyst and portfolio manager, and that in turn depends on an organization in which the analyst is not encouraged to exaggerate.

Notes

1. Managers sometimes describe any portfolio that includes bets on specific stocks as an active portfolio.

2. See chapter 10 for a further discussion of these possible tax effects.

3. The implications of this "single index" model for portfolio selection were first explored by Sharpe (3). Subsequently Treynor and Black (4) showed how selection of the equity portfolio could be divided into two stages.

4. If the passive portfolio moves closely with the market, we can split up the expected reward as follows: Expected reward = expected specific reward + beta × expected reward from passive portfolio. Thus, when you are forecasting the specific reward, you should focus on how well you would expect each stock to perform if the reward on the passive portfolio was zero.

5. Notice that pessimism about the market should not lead you to concentrate on low-beta stocks, nor should optimism cause you to prefer high-beta stocks. It is more effective to act directly on the proportion of your fund that is invested in the passive portfolio.

6. See Hodges (1). This assumes that there are no costs to moving back and forth between stocks and cash. In practice, therefore, you should make much smaller moves than this rule implies.

7. If you cannot sell short, the active portfolio will largely contain stocks that you think are undervalued. It will, therefore, give you a positive investment in the market. Even if you have only modest ability to pick stocks, the investment in the market will often be larger than you would like. In that case you would not want to invest anything in an index fund. You would like to reduce your investment in the market by selling index futures.

8. For a discussion of the problems of split funding, see Rosenberg (5) and Sharpe (6).

9. See Hodges and Brealey (2).

10. The forecasts in table 9.1 were exaggerated. The stocks with good prospects did not on average perform as well as expected, and those with poor prospects did not perform as badly as expected. Before the optimal portfolios were selected, the forecasts were adjusted to remove this exaggeration.

References

Some papers on portfolio selection:

(1) Hodges, S. D. "An Operational Model for Portfolio Selection." Ph.D. dissertation, University of London, 1973.

(2) Hodges, S. D., and Brealey, R. A. "Portfolio Selection in a Dynamic and Uncertain World." *Financial Analysts Journal* 29 (March–April 1973):50–66.

(3) Sharpe, W. F. "A Simplified Model for Portfolio Analysis." *Management Science* 9 (January 1963):277–293.

(4) Treynor, J. L., and Black, F. "How to Use Security Analysis to Improve Portfolio Selection." *Journal of Business* 46 (January 1973):66–86.

Two papers on "split funding":

(5) Rosenberg, B. *Institutional Investment Management with Multiple Portfolio Managers.* University of California, Berkeley, Institute of Business and Economic Research, working paper no. 65, October 1977.

(6) Sharpe, W. F. "Decentralized Investment Management." *Journal of Finance* 36 (May 1981):217–234.

10 Risk and Return

Investors are not obliged to take any risks. They can, if they choose, put all their money in a bank account and just receive a known rate of interest. Therefore, if investors dislike risk, they will invest in the stock market only if it offers the prospect of a higher return than safe alternatives.

This choice is illustrated in figure 10.1. An insured bank account is risk-free, so it has a beta of 0, and in exchange it pays a known rate of interest. By contrast, investment in a fully diversified portfolio of stocks has average risk, so its beta is 1.0. In exchange for bearing the risk of common stock investment, you can expect to receive a higher return than the rate of interest. Between 1926 and 1981 this difference between the market return and the interest rate averaged more than 8 percent a year, so we might judge that this is roughly the premium that investors have expected for taking on the risk of stock market investment.[1]

If you are prepared to incur a modest amount of risk, you can invest part of your money in a bank account and part in the stock market. For example, if you were to divide your money evenly between the two, your portfolio would have a beta of 0.5, and its expected return would be midway between the interest rate and the expected return on the market. In figure 10.2 we have shown this portfolio by the letter X.

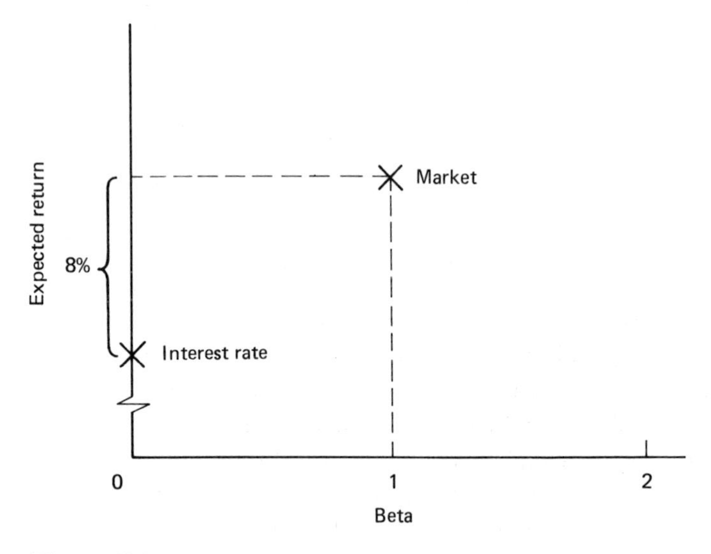

Figure 10.1
Investing in stocks is risky, but on past evidence you can expect an extra return of about 8 percent for taking this risk.

Alternatively, if you are courageous, you can borrow money from the bank and invest both this and your own funds in the stock market. For example, if you invested equal amounts of borrowed money and your own funds, your portfolio would have a beta of 2.0, and its expected return would be twice the expected market return less the interest rate. In figure 10.2 we have shown this portfolio by the letter Y.

These two examples illustrate a general point: By mixing an investment in the market with borrowing or lending, you can obtain any combination of risk and expected return along the sloping line in figure 10.2. This line is often known as the market line.

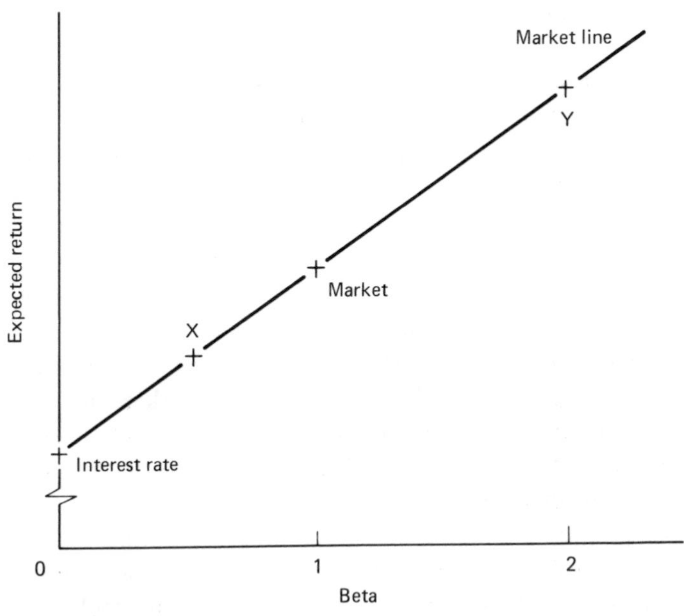

Figure 10.2
By investing some money in the market portfolio and borrowing or lending the balance, you can achieve any position along the market line.

Risk and Return from Individual Stocks

The market line does not just describe the expected return from investing a different fraction of your funds in the market; if there is competition between investors, it also describes the return that you can expect from particular stocks. For example, we saw in chapter 8 that on past evidence AT&T has a beta of 0.3. In other words, it has the same beta as a fund that has 30 percent of its money invested in the market portfolio and the remainder in a bank account. The market line tells us that if AT&T is fairly priced, it should offer the same expected return as this mixture of market portfolio and bank account.

We also saw in chapter 8 that on past evidence Zenith stock has a beta of 2.6. You could also have a beta of 2.6 by investing in the market portfolio $1.60 of borrowed money for each $1.00 of your own funds. Therefore, if Zenith stock is fairly priced, it should offer the same expected return as this levered investment in the market portfolio.

The return on the market portfolio is simply the average of the returns on individual stocks. Therefore, we know that on average expected returns must lie on the market line. The startling notion is that in competitive markets the expected return from each stock must also lie on the line. For example, consider what would happen if investors revised downward their forecast of AT&T's dividend growth. If the stock price did not change, the stock's expected return would now be less than the expected return on a comparable mixture of bank account and market portfolio. Thus it would lie below the market line. If investors were on their toes, such a situation could not persist. AT&T's stockholders would see that they could increase their expected return with no greater risk by selling their stock and investing the proceeds in a mixture of bank account and market portfolio. As a result, the stock price of AT&T would fall and the expected return would rise until it lies once again on the market line. Thus, in equilibrium, expected returns cannot be scattered around the market line; for each stock, the expected reward for risk must be proportional to its beta.

The idea that there exists a simple relationship between expected return and beta is generally referred to as the capital asset pricing model.[2] Underlying the model are two basic notions. The first is that investors do not like risk and therefore require the prospect of some additional reward for investing in risky securities. The second is the notion that this expected reward should be proportional to the risk that cannot be diversified away and is unaffected by the risk that can be avoided.

The capital asset pricing model describes the consensus view about each stock's return. If you share this view, you will believe that each stock simply offers a fair reward for risk. In this case the market portfolio is the efficient portfolio for you, and you should invest in the market whatever sum you are prepared to venture and borrow or lend the balance. If you have superior forecasting ability, you will occasionally disagree with the consensus. In this case you will want to take above-average positions in stocks that you believe lie above the market line and below-average positions in those that you believe lie below the line.

Dividends and Other Complications

The capital asset pricing model captures simply and elegantly the fundamental idea that investors need to be paid for taking on nondiversifiable risk. Underlying the model there are several assumptions that have not been spelled out. For example, it was implicitly assumed that investors can borrow at the same rate as they can lend. For large companies that is probably true, but it may not be so for everyone.[3] A second assumption was that all investments can be freely bought and sold. There are, however, many investments that are not marketable. For example, a person's most valuable possession is often his own talent, and this cannot easily be sold to others.[4]

A number of studies have looked at how such additional complications would affect the relationship between risk and expected return. For the portfolio manager, probably the most interesting of these studies are those concerned with the effect of taxes on risk and return.

The average investor pays a higher rate of tax on dividends than on capital gains. Therefore, he will not be prepared to hold stocks with a high dividend yield unless they also offer the compensation of a higher pretax return. In this case two stocks with the same level of market risk may offer different expected pretax returns to the average investor but should have the same expected return after tax.

This can have important implications for the type of portfolio that the investor should hold. If he pays tax at the average rate, then each stock will offer the prospect of a fair return after tax and he will be happy to hold the market portfolio. If he has the misfortune to be a millionaire and pays tax at an above-average rate, then stocks with a low dividend yield should provide a higher return after tax and the portfolio should have unusually large holdings in these stocks. On the other hand, if the portfolio is a pension fund that does not pay tax, then high yielding stocks are likely to provide the higher return and the portfolio should be concentrated in these stocks.[5]

Testing the Relationship between Risk and Return

Many of the simplest ideas in economics turn out to be the most difficult to test, and so it is with the capital asset pricing model. One of the principal problems is that we can never observe what returns investors expected to receive. Maybe over the long run investors get what they expect, but they certainly do not always do so in the short run. A second difficulty is that in principle the market portfolio contains all risky investments, but in practice stock market indexes measure the returns on only a sample of these investments.[6]

One way to test the model is first to estimate the betas of NYSE stocks using the returns in each odd month over a ten-year period.[7] The stocks can then be grouped into twenty portfolios on the basis of these estimated betas. Since the high betas are likely to be overestimated and the low betas are likely to be underestimated, the beta of each portfolio needs to be recalculated using the returns in each even month over the ten-year period. This provides a relatively unbiased and accurate estimate of the beta of each portfolio. The final step is to plot these portfolio betas against the portfolio returns in the subsequent five-year period.

Figure 10.3 shows the results of conducting such an exercise for NYSE stocks for the period 1935–1968. Notice that in most, but not all, periods the portfolio returns do indeed cluster around the market line. We do not know whether we should get a much better fit if we were able to measure expected returns rather than actual returns, and we do not know whether the fit would be better if the betas were measured against a different index. Thus we cannot be sure just how good an approximation the capital asset pricing model is.

Despite these reservations, figure 10.3 contains an important message for portfolio managers. If they estimate the beta of stocks relative to a stock market index, they will not only learn about how those stocks affect the risk of a diversified portfolio but will discover something about their likely return. Stocks with high estimated betas have subsequently had higher average returns than those with low estimated betas.

Studies of the capital asset pricing model indicate that average returns are related to beta, but some tests suggest that returns are related to other things as well. For example, there seems to be an important relationship between a company's size and the subsequent return on its stock. Suppose that between 1926 and 1981 you had held the NYSE stocks that were in the bottom 20 percent in terms of market capitalization. Your average return would have been 6.7 percent a year higher than that of Standard and Poor's Composite Index.[8] There is no good theory that links company size, liquidity, and expected returns, but if it is true that factors

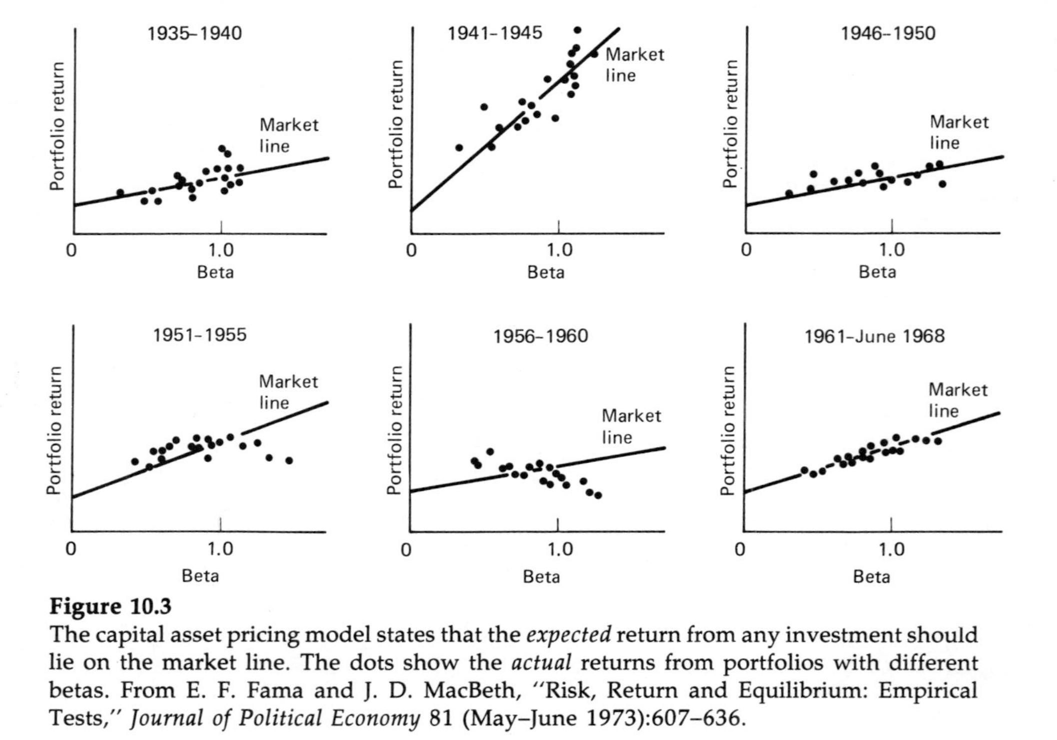

Figure 10.3
The capital asset pricing model states that the *expected* return from any investment should lie on the market line. The dots show the *actual* returns from portfolios with different betas. From E. F. Fama and J. D. MacBeth, "Risk, Return and Equilibrium: Empirical Tests," *Journal of Political Economy* 81 (May–June 1973):607–636.

other than beta command a premium, then the capital asset pricing model is not the whole truth.

Implications of the Capital Asset Pricing Model

The capital asset pricing model is concerned with how stocks are priced in well-functioning markets, and it does not say anything about how managers ought to act. Nevertheless, the model has some important implications for the portfolio manager. First, it is a reminder that in a competitive stock market the choice of a portfolio's risk is likely to have a much greater impact on its return than the manager's forecasting ability.

The second important lesson is that the manager should not expect to be compensated for the risk that can be diversified away. The only risk that he gets paid for taking is the kind that stems from broad market movements. This is measured by beta.

Notes

1. See Ibbotson and Sinquefield (31).

2. The capital asset pricing model was independently discovered by Lintner (2), Sharpe (4), and Treynor (5).

3. If borrowing and lending rates differ or there are restrictions on borrowing, then stocks should still lie on a market line, but this line passes through the expected return on the least variable zero beta portfolio rather than through the interest rate. See Black (6) and Brennan (7).

4. In this case the beta also depends on how the nonmarketable asset moves with other assets. See Mayers (9).

5. See Brennan (12). Some economists do not agree with Brennan that high yielding stocks sell at lower prices. They believe that if this were so, companies would not pay such high dividends. If these economists are right, high yielding stocks would offer lower

returns to any tax-paying investor. See, for example, Black and Scholes (10) and Miller and Scholes (17).

6. Some of the difficulties in testing the model have been analyzed by Miller and Scholes (23) and Roll (24).

7. See Fama and MacBeth (28).

8. See Ibbotson and Sinquefield (31). Part of this difference may be due to the higher betas of small company stocks.

References

Some classic papers on the capital asset pricing theory:

(1) Fama, E. F. "Risk, Return and Equilibrium." *Journal of Political Economy* 79 (January–February 1971):30–55.

(2) Lintner, J. "The Valuation of Risk Assets and the Selection of Risky Investments in Stock Portfolios and Capital Budgets." *Review of Economics and Statistics* 47 (February 1965):13–37.

(3) Mossin, J. "Equilibrium in a Capital Asset Market." *Econometrica* 34 (October 1966):768–783.

(4) Sharpe, W. F. "Capital Asset Prices: A Theory of Market Equilibrium under Conditions of Risk." *Journal of Finance* 19 (September 1964):425–442

(5) Treynor, J. L. "Towards a Theory of Market Value of Risky Assets." Unpublished manuscript, 1961.

The papers by Black, Brennan, and Mayers describe some elaborations to the capital asset pricing model. Other suggested modifications are reviewed by Jensen:

(6) Black, F. "Capital Market Equilibrium with Restricted Borrowing." *Journal of Business* 45 (July 1972):444–454.

(7) Brennan, M. J. "Capital Market Equilibrium with Divergent Borrowing and Lending Rates." *Journal of Financial and Quantitative Analysis* 6 (December 1971):1197–1205.

(8) Jensen, M. C. "Capital Markets Theory and Evidence." *Bell Journal of Economics and Management Science* 3 (Autumn 1972):357–398.

(9) Mayers, D. "Non-marketable Assets and Capital Market Equilibrium." In Jensen, M. C., ed., *Studies in the Theory of Capital Markets*. New York: Praeger Publishers, 1972.

Some studies of the effect of dividend yield on expected returns:

(10) Black, F., and Scholes, M. "The Effects of Dividend Yield and Dividend Policy on Common Stock Prices and Returns." *Journal of Financial Economics* 1 (May 1974):1–22.

(11) Blume, M. E. "Stock Returns and Dividend Yields: Some More Evidence." Unpublished paper, October 1978.

(12) Brennan, M. J. "Taxes, Market Valuation and Corporate Financial Policy." *National Tax Journal* 23 (1970):417–427.

(13) Elton, E. J., and Gruber, M. J. "Marginal Stockholder Tax Rates and the Clientele Effect." *Review of Economics and Statistics* 52 (February 1970):68–74.

(14) Hess, P. J. "The Empirical Relationship between Dividend Yields and Stock Returns: Tax Effects or Nonstationarities in Expected Returns." Unpublished paper, Ohio State University, October 1979.

(15) Litzenberger, R. H., and Ramaswamy, K. "Dividends, Short Selling Restrictions, Tax-Induced Investor Clienteles and Market Equilibrium." *Journal of Finance* 35 (May 1980):469–481.

(16) Litzenberger, R. H., and Ramaswamy, K. "The Effect of Personal Taxes and Dividends on Capital Asset Prices." *Journal of Financial Economics* 7 (June 1979):163–195.

(17) Miller, M. H., and Scholes, M. "Dividends and Taxes." *Journal of Financial Economics* 6 (December 1978):333–364.

(18) Miller, M. H., and Scholes, M. "Dividends and Taxes: Empirical Evidence." Unpublished paper, University of Chicago, Graduate School of Business, 1980.

(19) Sharpe, W. F., and Sosin, H. B. "Risk, Return and Yield, New York Stock Exchange Common Stocks, 1928–1969." *Financial Analysts Journal* 32 (March–April 1976):33–42.

The following papers examine the relationship between returns and firm size:

(20) Banz, R. W. "The Relationship Between Return and Market Value of Common Stocks." *Journal of Financial Economics* 9 (March 1981):3–18.

(21) Reinganum, M. R. "Misspecification of Capital Asset Pricing: Empirical Anomalies Based on Earnings' Yields and Market Values." *Journal of Financial Economics* 9 (March 1981):19–46.

Ross's paper suggests an alternative model of prices in which a number of factors may earn a risk premium:

(22) Ross, S. A. "The Arbitrage Theory of Capital Asset Pricing." *Journal of Economic Theory* 13 (1976):341–360.

These papers provide a critical analysis of the capital asset pricing model and its testability:

(23) Miller, M. H., and Scholes, M. "Rates of Return in Relationship to Risk: A Re-examination of Some Recent Findings." In Jensen, M. C., ed., *Studies in the Theory of Capital Markets.* New York: Praeger Publishers, 1972.

(24) Roll, R. "A Critique of the Asset Pricing Theory's Tests; Part 1: On Past and Potential Testability of the Theory." *Journal of Financial Economics* 4 (March 1977):129–176.

(25) Ross, S. A. "The Current Status of the CAPM." *Journal of Finance* 33 (June 1978):885–890.

Some tests of the capital asset pricing model:

(26) Black, F., Jensen, M. C., and Scholes, M. "The Capital Asset Pricing Model, Some Empirical Tests." In Jensen, M. C., ed., *Studies in the Theory of Capital Markets.* New York: Praeger Publishers, 1972.

(27) Blume, M. E., and Friend, I. "A New Look at the Capital Asset Pricing Model." *Journal of Finance* 28 (January 1973):19–33.

(28) Fama, E. F., and MacBeth, J. D. "Risk, Return and Equilibrium: Empirical Tests." *Journal of Political Economy* 81 (May–June 1973):607–636.

(29) Rosenberg, V., and Marathe, V. "Tests of Capital Asset Pricing Hypotheses." Unpublished paper, University of California, Berkeley, 1975.

(30) Sharpe, W. F., and Cooper, G. M. "Risk-Return Classes of New York Stock Exchange Stocks, 1931–1967." *Financial Analysts Journal* 28 (March–April 1972):46–54.

Ibbotson and Sinquefield provide some data on average historical returns from common stocks:

(31) Ibbotson, R. G., and Sinquefield, R. A. "Stocks, Bonds, Bills and Inflation: The Past and the Future." Charlottesville, Va., Financial Analysts Research Foundation, 1982.

11 Measuring Investment Performance

If you are paying a large fee to an investment manager, it makes sense to monitor whether he is earning his money. Even if you have no worries on that score, it may still be helpful to diagnose the manager's relative strengths and weaknesses. That is why performance measurement has become such a popular pastime.

The problem with performance measurement is that it is very difficult to distinguish whether the investment results were due to skill or chance. Consequently, however careful your assessment of the manager's record, you are likely to have only the most tenuous indication of the portfolio's likely performance in the future.

This means that it is not sufficient to measure the manager's performance; you also need to judge how much weight to place on the results. The investment manager who is dogged by constant homilies on his short-run performance is scarcely likely to make wise investment decisions.

Measuring Returns

The first step in performance measurement is to calculate the portfolio returns. If no new cash has been invested in the fund, this is a simple matter. You just sum the dividend receipts and the capital appreciation and divide the total by the initial market value of the fund.

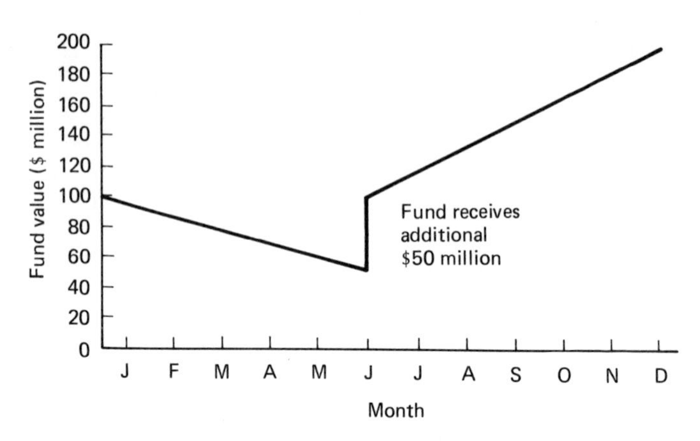

Figure 11.1
When a fund receives new cash, you need to be careful how you measure return. On one definition this fund gave a 40 percent return; on another definition the return was 0 percent.

The problems arise when there are cash flows into or out of the fund. For example, consider the hypothetical index fund in figure 11.1. The fund has an initial investment of $100 million. In the first six months the index falls by 50 percent, leaving the fund with a market value of $50 million. At this point the fund receives an additional $50 million to invest in the index. During the next six months the market exactly recovers its earlier decline, and the fund ends the year with a market value of $200 million.

One possible measure of the fund's return is the "discounted cash flow," or "internal" rate of return. In the case of our index fund, the internal rate of return is approximately 40 percent a year. In other words, $100 million invested for a year at 40 percent and $50 million invested for six months at the same rate would provide a final value of $200 million.

Now there is something odd about the notion that our index fund was able to earn a return of 40 percent in a year that the index was unchanged. The reason for this is that the internal rate of return is influenced by the timing of the cash flow. Because the index fund received new cash during a temporary dip in the market, the fund had a higher rate of return than the index itself. If the cash had arrived during a temporary rise, the fund would have had a lower internal rate of return than the index. As long as the arrival of these cash flows is beyond the manager's control, the internal rate of return cannot be used to judge his performance.

An alternative measure of a fund's return is the so-called "time-weighted" rate of return. This gives equal weight to each time period regardless of the amount of new money that is invested. For example, in the case of our hypothetical index fund, an initial investment of one dollar would have fallen in value to fifty cents by the end of the first half-year; by the end of the second half-year this investment of fifty cents would have appreciated again to one dollar. The time-weighted return is simply the return on the initial investment of one dollar; in our example, this return was exactly zero.

To calculate the time-weighted rate of return, we simply followed through the fortunes of an investment of one dollar in the fund. But to do this, we needed to know the value of the fund at the time that new cash was invested in the fund. In practice investment firms do not value their funds every day, so it is usually necessary to estimate the value of the fund at the time of the new cash flow. One solution is to pretend that the fund appreciated at a constant rate throughout the period, but you can generally get a better estimate than this by using your knowledge of the level of the market at the time of the cash flow.[1]

Choosing a Benchmark

Once you have measured the portfolio's time-weighted rate of return, you need to judge whether this return is satisfactory. In order to do that, you need a benchmark. In choosing a benchmark, it is essential to compare like with like. For example, you would not conclude that the manager of a corporate bond portfolio had done a good job just because his portfolio had earned a higher yield than Treasury bonds. Corporate bonds are more risky than Treasuries, and you would expect them to offer a higher yield. In just the same way you should not directly compare the return on two common stock portfolios with different degrees of risk.

In earlier chapters we saw that much of the risk of an individual stock can be diversified away. Therefore, the effect of a stock on the risk of a well-diversified portfolio depends not on whether that stock is individually very risky but on the extent to which it is affected by market movements. This sensitivity to market movements is measured by beta.

Suppose that over the past five years the interest rate has averaged 10 percent and the return on the market index has averaged 16 percent a year. The sloping line in figure 11.2 shows the different combinations of return and beta that you could have obtained by changing the proportion of your money that was invested in the market index. Here are four possible strategies:

Safe strategy: If you had invested none of your money in the index, your portfolio would have had a beta of 0 and you would just have earned the interest rate of 10 percent.

Low-risk strategy: If you had placed half your money in the market, your portfolio would have had a beta of 0.5 and its return would have been halfway between the return on the index and the interest rate.

Average-risk strategy: By investing all your money in the market, you would have had a beta of 1.0 and you would have received the market return of 16 percent.

High-risk strategy: By investing equal amounts of your own money and borrowed money in the market, the beta of your

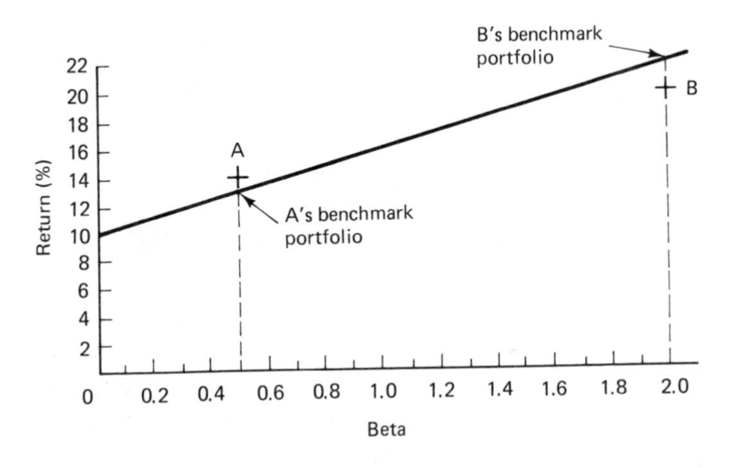

Figure 11.2
The return on fund A was 1 percent higher than on a benchmark portfolio with similar market risk. The return on fund B was 1 percent lower than on its benchmark portfolio.

investment would have increased to 2.0 and the return would have increased to 22 percent.

None of these strategies would have required any skill; they could have been followed by the greenest of greenhorns. Thus the sloping line in figure 11.2 serves as a useful standard against which to judge a professional manager. For example, portfolio A in figure 11.2 had a beta of 0.5. Therefore, its market risk was less than the average. Although the return was also below average, it was nonetheless about 1 percent a year more than you could have gotten by following a naive strategy with the same market risk. Therefore, A's stock selection must have increased the annual return by 1 percent.[2]

A Second Benchmark

In the last section we saw that manager A's stock selection produced an extra return of 1 percent a year. But you cannot both beat the market and hold the market. In order to obtain that extra return, A must have taken on some additional diversifiable risk.

If manager A is responsible for only a small part of a much larger portfolio, it may not matter that his portion of the portfolio is poorly diversified. If he is managing the entire pension fund, you may wish to examine whether his gain from picking stocks more than compensated for the additional risk that could have been diversified away.

The correlation between portfolio A's return and the market return measures how well A was diversified. If this correlation is much less than 1.0, then you know that A incurred significant diversifiable risk.

We have already seen how you could have achieved the same *market* risk as A by investing a proportion of your funds in the market and the remainder in Treasury bills. You could also have achieved the same *total* risk as A by choosing a different combination of the market and bills. In this case the proportion of your money that you would have needed to invest in the market is equal to the beta of A's portfolio divided by the correlation between the portfolio and the market. For example, suppose that this correlation was 0.8. Then you could have matched A's total risk by investing 0.5/0.8 or 63 percent of your portfolio in the market. Figure 11.3 shows that, if you had done so, your return would have been almost the same as A's. Evidently A's gains from stock selection were almost exactly counterbalanced by the portfolio's diversifiable risk.[3]

Problems with Performance Measurement

To measure manager A's performance, we compared the return on his portfolio with the return on two benchmark portfolios. When we wanted to know whether A had made any gains from stock selection, we looked at a benchmark

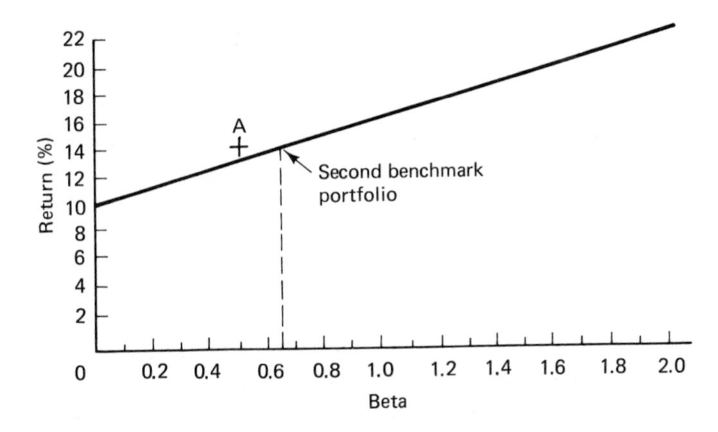

Figure 11.3
The return on fund A is similar to the return on a second benchmark portfolio that has the same *total* risk.

portfolio that had the same market risk as A. When we considered whether the gains from stock selection compensated for the additional diversifiable risk, we looked at a portfolio that had the same total risk as A.

In choosing these benchmark portfolios, it is important not only that a naive investor could hold them but that it would be sensible for him to do so.[4] If we judge a manager's performance against an inefficient benchmark portfolio, then a naive manager may be able to find a strategy that is likely to beat the benchmark. There is some evidence that a mixture of Treasury bills and a market index is not a perfect benchmark. For example, it seems to have flattered the performance of those managers who have invested in low-beta stocks or in small companies.[5] But, despite these reservations, the fact that professional managers find it so difficult to beat a mixture of bills and market index suggests that it is not a bad yardstick against which to judge them.[6]

There are two ways to beat the market: one can be skillful or one can be lucky. Unfortunately, it is not easy to distinguish the skillful managers from the lucky ones just by looking at portfolio performance. The problem is that you need to measure the manager's performance over a very long period before you can be sure that his gains are more than a coincidence. For example, we saw in chapter 9 that even when the manager has only modest forecasting ability, a well-constructed portfolio can beat the market by an average of 1 percent a year. Such a portfolio would be subject to periodic spells of good or ill fortune, and as a result it would be at least twenty-five years before you could be 95 percent sure that the manager did truly have some superior ability.[7]

This does not imply that you should not measure a manager's performance until he has been in the business for twenty-five years. It does mean that you should look not only at the gains that the manager has made in the past but at the probability that these gains were more than a coincidence. Performance measurers have an incentive not to give you this information; they would like you to believe that they are always measuring true differences in skill.

The second and more important message is that you should be cautious about the reliance you place on performance measures. It may sound like good practice to give most of your funds to the manager with the best performance, but in reality that usually amounts to giving them to the one who was luckiest. Therefore, do not focus on past performance to the exclusion of other information. No matter how good a manager's recent performance, if he seems like a bungling amateur, he probably is one.

Notes

1. These alternative ways to estimate the time-weighted rate of return are described by the Bank Administration Institute (1).

2. This measure of the gain from stock selection is sometimes referred to as "alpha." It was originally suggested by Jensen (3).

3. This measure of performance was suggested by Sharpe (4). A useful discussion of the components of performance is given in Fama (2).

4. For a discussion of this point, see Roll (7, 8, 9).

5. The fact that these performance measures may be biased in favor of low-beta portfolios was suggested by Friend and Blume (6). See the references to chapter 10 for evidence on the apparently high returns on small company shares.

6. It is important, however, to look out for the exceptions. For example, you should compare the performance of an internationally diversified portfolio against a sensible passive portfolio, not against the Standard and Poor's index.

7. See Hodges and Brealey (10).

References

This standard text on performance measurement contains a chapter on estimating time-weighted returns:

(1) Bank Administration Institute. *Measuring the Investment Performance of Pension Funds*. Park Ridge, Ill.: Bank Administration Institute, 1968.

These papers discuss the choice of an appropriate benchmark:

(2) Fama, E. F. "Components of Investment Performance." *Journal of Finance* 27 (June 1972):551–568.

(3) Jensen, M. C. "Risk, the Pricing of Capital Assets and the Evaluation of Investment Portfolios." *Journal of Business* 62 (April 1969):167–247.

(4) Sharpe, W. F. "Mutual Fund Performance." *Journal of Business* 39 (January 1966):119–138.

(5) Treynor, J. L. "How to Rate Management of Investment Funds." *Harvard Business Review* 43 (January–February 1965):63–75.

These papers illustrate some problems with the choice of a performance benchmark:

(6) Friend, I., and Blume, M. E. "Measurement of Portfolio Performance under Uncertainty." *American Economic Review* 60 (September 1970):561–575.

(7) Roll, R. "Ambiguity When Performance is Measured by the Security Market Line." *Journal of Finance* 33 (September 1978):1051–1069.

(8) Roll, R. "Performance Evaluation and Benchmark Errors." *Journal of Portfolio Management* 7 (Summer 1980):5–12.

(9) Roll, R. "Performance Evaluation and Benchmark Errors II." *Journal of Portfolio Management* 8 (Winter 1981):17–22.

This paper shows that it can be difficult to distinguish skill from good luck:

(10) Hodges, S. D., and Brealey, R. A. "Portfolio Selection in a Dynamic and Uncertain World." *Financial Analysts Journal* 29 (March–April 1973):50–66.

This paper develops significance tests of performance:

(11) Jobson, J. D., and Korkie, R. M. "Performance Testing with the Sharpe and Treynor Measures." *Journal of Finance* 36 (September 1981):889–908.

Name Index

Mentions in end-of-chapter notes or references are indicated by italics. The remaining entries refer to the main text.

Subject Index